MOON

NEWFOUNDLAND & LABRADOR

ANDREW HEMPSTEAD

D1417104

Contents

St. John's and the Avalon Peninsula

S t. John's, the provincial capital, is a colorful and comfortable city. Situated on the steep inland side of St. John's Harbour, the city's rooftops form a tapestry: Some are gracefully drawn with swooping mansard curves, some are

pancake-flat or starkly pitched, and others are pyramidal with clay pots placed atop the central chimneys. Against this otherwise picture-perfect tapestry, the tangle of electrical wires strung up and down the hillside is a visual offense.

Contrasts of color are everywhere. House windows are framed in deep turquoise, red, bright yellow, or pale pink and are covered with starched white lace curtains. Window boxes are stuffed to overflowing with red geraniums and purple and pink petunias. Along the streets, cement walls brace the hillside, and any blank surface serves as an excuse for a pastel-painted mural. The storefronts on Water Street, as individual as their owners, stand out in Wedgwood blue, lime green, purple, and rose. At streetside, public telephone booths are painted the bright red of old-time fire hydrants.

As the Newfoundlanders say, St. John's offers the best for visitors—another way of saying that Newfoundland is short on cities and

long on coastal outports. But without question, St. John's thrives with places for dining, nightlife, sightseeing, and lodging—more than anywhere else across the island and Labrador. Simply put, the Newfoundlanders have carved a contemporary, livable, and intriguing niche in one of North America's most ancient ports. Come to St. John's for some of Atlantic Canada's most abundant high-quality shopping, unusual dining in lush surroundings, interesting maritime history displayed in fine museums, rousing nightlife and music, and an emerging and eclectic fine-arts scene.

When you're done with the city, there's the rest of the Avalon Peninsula to discover. Within day-tripping distance of downtown, you can go whale-watching at Witless Bay Ecological Reserve, watch archaeologists at work at Ferryland, walk in to North America's most accessible bird sanctuary at Cape St. Mary's, and drive through delightfully named villages like Heart's Desire.

Previous: St. John's Harbour; Gower Street is lined with colorful homes. **Above:** Witless Bay.

6

Look for ★ to find recommended
sights, activities, dining, and lodging.

Highlights

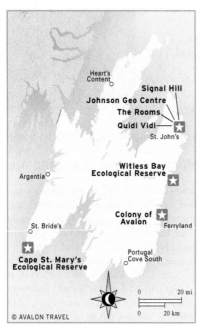

© AVALON TRAVEL

★ **The Rooms:** A museum, an art gallery, and spectacular harbor views are wrapped up together in this magnificent complex showcasing the very best of everything in Newfoundland and Labrador (page 9).

★ **Signal Hill:** The sweeping ocean and city views alone make the drive to the top of Signal Hill worthwhile (page 13).

★ **Johnson Geo Centre:** Descend underground in a glass-sided elevator at this Signal Hill attraction, where the ancient geological world of the province comes to life (page 14).

★ **Quidi Vidi:** With its charming fishing shacks and rugged shoreline, you could be in a Newfoundland "outport" (remote fishing village), but you're not—downtown is just over the hill (page 15).

★ **Witless Bay Ecological Reserve:** Jump aboard a tour boat and head out to this reserve, where you're almost guaranteed whale, puffin, and seal sightings (page 31).

★ **Colony of Avalon:** Integrated with the seaside village of Ferryland, this ongoing archaeological dig is slowly uncovering one of North America's oldest European settlements (page 32).

★ **Cape St. Mary's Ecological Reserve:** Even if you have no real interest in birds, the sights and sounds of thousands of gannets on this offshore rock stack are a spectacle to remember (page 34).

St. John's and the Avalon Peninsula

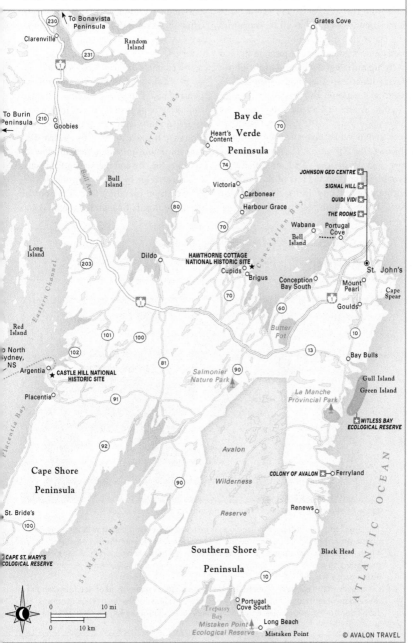

© AVALON TRAVEL

PLANNING YOUR TIME

Whether you arrive by air, by ferry, or overland from the west, St. John's is a definite destination in itself. It has all the amenities of a major city, including top-notch accommodations, a good range of restaurants, and lively nightlife. Sightseeing will easily fill two days, with at least a few hours spent at The Rooms, a museum and art gallery complex as good as any in Canada. Don't miss the drive up to Signal Hill National Historic Site, and stop at Johnson Geo Centre along the way. The Fluvarium is a good rainy-day diversion. While the village of Quidi Vidi provides a taste of the rest of the province without leaving city limits, the rest of the Avalon Peninsula is well worth exploring.

The options are relatively straightforward—either use St. John's as a base for day trips or plan on an overnight excursion. Two highlights—a whale-watching trip to Witless Bay Ecological Reserve and a visit to the historic Colony of Avalon—can easily be combined into a day trip. Bird-rich Cape St. Mary's Ecological Reserve is also within a couple of hours' drive of St. John's, although if you're arriving by ferry from Nova Scotia, it's only a short detour from the main route into town. If you're arriving by air, five days is the minimum amount of time to allow for exploring the city and the Avalon Peninsula. If you're arriving by ferry with your own vehicle, plan on spending three days on the Avalon Peninsula (including St. John's) and

The Newfoundland Dog and Labrador Retriever

statues of a Labrador retriever and a Newfoundland dog in Harborside Park

The large long-haired Newfoundland dog is believed to have originated with the early Portuguese, who brought mountain sheepdogs across the Atlantic with them. Considered one of North America's finest show dogs, the Newfoundland is better known locally as a working dog. Its swimming prowess, used to rescue shipwrecked fishers and sailors from stormy seas, has inspired local legends.

Contrary to the name, the Labrador retriever originated on the island of Newfoundland as a descendant of the Newfoundland dog. The retriever was known as the "lesser Newfoundland," "St. John's dog," or "St. John's water dog" until its debut in London at the English Kennel Club in 1903.

seven days traveling through the central and western portion of the province to the ferry terminal at Port-aux-Basques. Add two days' travel from Halifax (including the two ferry trips from and to Sydney) and you can create a 12-day itinerary with no backtracking.

HISTORY

St. John's officially dates to 1497, when Newfoundlanders say the explorer John Cabot sailed into the harbor and claimed the area for England. By the early 1540s, St. John's Harbour was a major port on old-world maps, and the French explorer Jacques Cartier anchored there for ship repairs. The British—who arrived, conquered, and remained for centuries—have had the greatest impact here. By 1528 the port had its first residence, and the main lanes were the Lower Path (Water Street) and Upper Path (Duckworth Street). Fishing thrived, but settlement was slow. Early on, the defenseless port was easy game for other European imperialists, and in 1665 the Dutch plundered the town. Nevertheless, by 1675, St. John's had a population of 185, as well as 155 cattle and 48 boats anchored at 23 piers. By 1696, the French emerged as England's persistent adversary. The French launched destructive attacks on St. John's in 1696, 1705, and 1709.

St. John's was a seamy port through most of its early years. In a town bereft of permanent settlement and social constraints, 80 taverns and innumerable brothels flourished on Water Street, with a few stores on Duckworth Street and Buckleys Lane (George Street). The port's inhabitants were a motley mix of Spaniards, Portuguese, French, and British; as the latter gained dominance, Anglo immigration was encouraged. In 1892, a huge fire destroyed the city from Water Street to the East End, leveling 1,572 houses and 150 stores and leaving 1,900 families homeless. The stores, commercial buildings, and merchant mansions were re-created in Gothic Revival and Second Empire styles.

Sights

Most of St. John's best sightseeing revolves around the city's long and colorful history. In addition to traditional sights such as The Rooms (the provincial museum) and national historic sites, go beyond the ordinary and plan on sipping a pint of beer at the Crow's Nest and joining a guided walking tour of downtown—both excellent ways to soak up the seafaring ambience of this historic city.

DOWNTOWN

Although adding to the charm in many ways, the layout of downtown defies modern logic. The streets follow footpaths laid out by European fishermen and sailors centuries ago, when towns were not planned but simply evolved for everyone's convenience. Water Street (one of North America's oldest streets) and the other main streets rise parallel to the waterfront and are intersected by roads meandering across the hillside. Historic stone staircases climb grades too steep for paved roads.

★ The Rooms

One of Canada's finest cultural facilities, The Rooms (9 Bonaventure Ave., 709/757-8000; June-mid-Oct. Mon.-Sat. 10am-5pm and Sun. noon-5pm, mid-Oct.-May Tues.-Sat. 10am-5pm and Wed.-Thurs. until 9pm; adult $7.50, senior $5, child $4) combines a provincial museum, art gallery, and archives under one roof. Styled on the simple oceanfront "fishing rooms" where Newfoundlanders would process their catch, this complex setting on the site of a 1750s fort is anything but basic. From a distance, it is nothing short of spectacular to see the ultramodern "rooms" rising above the rest of the city like a mirage. The interior is no

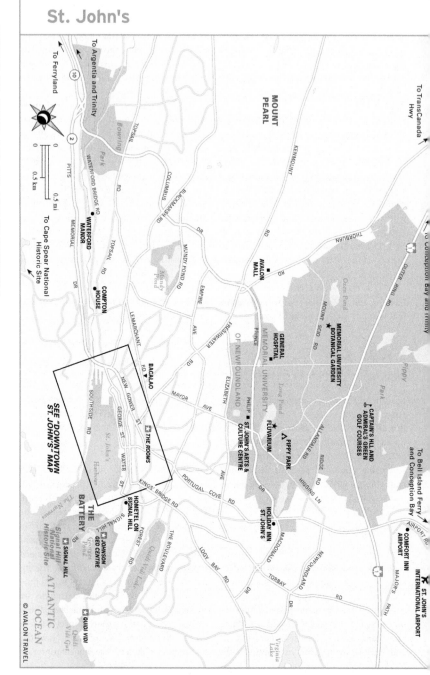

St. John's

To Ferryland

To Argentia and Trinity

To TransCanada Hwy

10

2

To Conception Bay and Trinity

To Cape Spear National Historic Site

0   0.5 mi

0   0.5 km

MOUNT PEARL

WATERFORD MANOR

COMPTON HOUSE

Bowring Park

Waterford Bridge Rd

PITTS

MEMORIAL DR

TOPSAIL RD

TOPSAIL RD

COLUMBUS DR

BLACKMARSH RD

MUNDY POND RD

EMPIRE AVE

FRESHWATER RD

LEMARCHANT RD

NEW GOWER ST

GEORGE ST

WATER ST

SOUTHSIDE RD

Mundy Pond

KENMOUNT RD

MOUNT SCIO RD

OUTER RING RD

THORBURN

Oxen Pond

MEMORIAL UNIVERSITY OF NEWFOUNDLAND

PRINCE PHILIP DR

ELIZABETH AVE

MAYOR AVE

AVALON MALL

GENERAL HOSPITAL

MEMORIAL UNIVERSITY BOTANICAL GARDEN

CAPTAIN'S HILL AND ADMIRAL'S GREEN GOLF COURSES

Long Pond

Pippy Park

ALLANDALE RD

RIDGE RD

HIGGINS LN

PIPPY PARK

FLUVARIUM

ST. JOHN'S ARTS & CULTURE CENTRE

PORTUGAL COVE RD

KINGS BRIDGE RD

SIGNAL HILL RD

FOREST RD

THE BOULEVARD

LOGY BAY RD

MACDONALD DR

TORBAY RD

NEWFOUNDLAND DR

MAJOR'S PATH

AIRPORT RD

To Bell Island Ferry and Conception Bay

ST. JOHN'S INTERNATIONAL AIRPORT

COMFORT INN AIRPORT

BACALAO

THE ROOMS

SEE "DOWNTOWN ST. JOHN'S" MAP

St. John's Harbour

THE BATTERY

The Narrows

Signal Hill National Historic Site

SIGNAL HILL

JOHNSON GEO CENTRE

George's Pond

HOMETEL ON SIGNAL HILL

HOLIDAY INN ST. JOHN'S

Quidi Vidi Lake

QUIDI VIDI

Quidi Vidi Gut

Virginia Lake

ATLANTIC OCEAN

© AVALON TRAVEL

Downtown St. John's

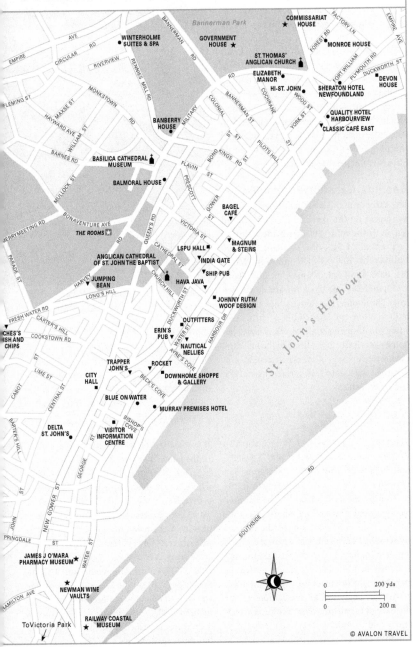

© AVALON TRAVEL

less impressive, with huge windows allowing uninterrupted views across the city and harbor. Displays in the museum component encompass the entire natural and human history of Newfoundland and Labrador, from glaciation to modern-day cultural diversity. The art gallery spreads across two floors. More than 7,000 works of art are displayed, with touring exhibits adding to the artistic mix. If you're a history buff with time to spare, include a visit to the archives, which contain more than 500,000 historic photos, plus government and shipping records, maps and atlases, family histories, and personal diaries.

Basilica Cathedral Museum

The early Roman Catholics aimed to make an impact on the skyline of St. John's, and did so in the mid-1800s with the Basilica Cathedral of St. John the Baptist (200 Military Rd., 709/754-2170; June-Sept. Mon.-Fri. 8am-4pm, Sat. 10am-5pm, Sun. 8am-12:30pm; free), one block toward downtown from The Rooms. The Romanesque cathedral, built of stone and shaped like a Latin cross with twin 43-meter-high towers, is now a national historic site. In addition to the museum, guided tours point out the ornate ceilings embellished with gold leaf, numerous statues, and other features.

Anglican Cathedral of St. John the Baptist

The Anglican Cathedral of St. John the Baptist (16 Church Hill, 709/726-5677; mid-June-Sept. Mon.-Fri. 10am-4pm, Sat. 10am-noon; free) is a national historic site revered by locals (and said to be haunted by a resident ghost). English architect Sir George Gilbert Scott designed the impressive Gothic Revival edifice in Newfoundland bluestone. The cornerstone was laid in 1847, and the Great Fire of 1892 almost gutted the structure. Reconstruction within the walls started the next year. Of special interest are the carved furnishings and sculpted arches and a gold communion service presented by King William IV.

The Rooms is St. John's premier cultural attraction.

James J. O'Mara Pharmacy Museum

Inside the splendidly restored and gleaming Apothecary Hall, the James J. O'Mara Pharmacy Museum (488 Water St., 709/753-5877; Mon.-Fri. 8am-4:30pm; free) recalls a pharmacy of 1895.

Newman Wine Vaults

In the late 1700s, wine that had been stored in St. John's was transported back to London, where it was deemed to have a much improved flavor. As a result, a number of wine vaults were constructed in the city, and cases of wine were brought across the Atlantic to mature. The last remaining of these is Newman Wine Vaults (436 Water St., 709/739-7870; July-Aug. Wed.-Sun. 9:30am-5pm; adult $6, senior $4, child $3), on the west side of downtown. Ensconced in a more modern shell, the two vaults, held together by mortar from crushed seashells, are the oldest buildings in St. John's.

Railway Coastal Museum

The Newfoundland Railway was a vital link for islanders between 1898 and the last scheduled passenger service in 1969. It extended the length of the island (roughly following the modern-day TransCanada Highway), terminating in the east at what is now the Railway Coastal Museum (495 Water St. W., 709/753-5877; summer daily 10am-5pm, fall-spring Tues.-Sun. 10am-5pm; adult $6, senior $5, child $4). Symbolizing the grandeur of its one-time importance, the city's main railway station forms the backbone of the museum, with historic photographs and memorabilia from days gone by. It is west of the New Gower Street overpass.

Government House

One of few structures that escaped damage in the Great Fire of 1892, Government House (50 Military Rd.; grounds open daily dawn-dusk) is the residence of the province's lieutenant governor. The impressive 1831 building was constructed of red sandstone quarried from Signal Hill and features a moat, ceiling frescoes, and flower gardens. This, the Commissariat House, and St. Thomas's Anglican Church are on the northern edge of downtown, a steep five-block walk from the waterfront.

Commissariat House

Now protected as a provincial historic site, the three-story Commissariat House (King's Bridge Rd., 709/729-6370; mid-May-early Oct. Wed.-Sun. 9:30am-5pm; adult $6, senior $4, child $3) began in 1818 as a residence and office for Fort William's assistant commissary general. Over the years, it was used as the St. Thomas's Church rectory, a nursing home, and a hospital. The interior, furnished with antiques, has been restored in the style of the 1830s.

St. Thomas's Anglican Church

St. Thomas's Anglican Church (corner of King's Bridge Rd. and Military Rd., 709/576-6632; free) is known as the Old Garrison Church. Dating to the 1830s, the city's oldest church houses a cast-iron Hanoverian coat of arms over the door, attesting to the royal lineage. Call for details of summer sanctuary tours.

★ SIGNAL HILL

The distinct geological feature of the Signal Hill National Historic Site rises high above the Narrows, at the mouth of St. John's Harbour. On a clear day, it's plainly visible from throughout town, but more importantly,

the view looking out from Signal Hill

it offers stunning views back across the city, down the coast, and out into the Atlantic Ocean. Although Signal Hill is only a little over two kilometers from the city center, it's a steep walk, so plan on driving.

★ Johnson Geo Centre

What better place for a geology museum than underground? Access to the Johnson Geo Centre (175 Signal Hill Rd., 709/724-7625; daily 9:30am-5pm; adult $12, senior $9, child $6), almost at the top of Signal Hill, is a glass-sided elevator that descends below the rocky landscape to a cavernous room where one entire wall exposes the 550-million-year-old bedrock. Displays describe the entire geological history of the province, from the oldest rocks on earth to modern oil and gas exploration. Highlights include a *Titanic* room, where you can watch footage from exploration of the famous wreck.

Signal Hill National Historic Site

In the 1700s, this hill, once known as the Lookout, served as part of a British signaling system; news of friendly or hostile ships was flagged from Cape Spear to Signal Hill, where the message was conveyed to Fort William in town. In 1762 the Battle of Signal Hill marked the Seven Years' War's final North American land battle, with England victorious and France the loser.

On the road up to the hilltop is the Visitor Interpretation Centre (709/772-5367; mid-May-mid-June Wed.-Sun. 10am-5pm, mid-June-Aug. daily 10am-5pm, Sept.-mid-Oct. Wed.-Sun. 10am-5pm; adult $4, senior $3.50, child $2), which tells the long and colorful story of Signal Hill through modern and interactive exhibits.

Continuing upwards by road or on foot, Cabot Tower (mid-Apr.-mid-Nov. daily 9am-5pm; Interpretation Centre admission includes Cabot Tower) is at the very top of Signal Hill. This is where Guglielmo Marconi received the first transatlantic wireless message. The hilltop is pocked with historical remnants. England's Imperial Powder Magazine stored gunpowder during the Napoleonic Wars, and the Queen's Battery—an authentic outpost tucked beneath the cliff—guarded the harbor Narrows from 1833.

For hiking, the North Head Trail peels off the top of the hill and follows the cliffs to Fort Chain Rock. The Cuckold's Cove Trail wends across Signal Hill's leeward side to Quidi Vidi Village.

Johnson Geo Centre

★ QUIDI VIDI

The Atlantic's watery inroads permeate the St. John's area. Aside from the city's famed harbor, another sizable pocket of the sea—Quidi Vidi Lake—lies nearby. Its azure-blue waters meet a boulder-bound coastline, all within the bustling city limits. Quidi Vidi Lake ("kiddie viddie" is the local pronunciation) is best known as the site of the Royal St. John's Regatta, held on the first Wednesday in August. The lake's choppy water also lures windsurfers. Locals enjoy strolls along the grassy banks. To get there, follow Water Street west under Pitts Memorial Drive and turn left onto Route 11 (Blackhead Road).

Beyond the lake is picturesque Quidi Vidi Village. Wander the narrow winding streets of this fishing village, and you'll never believe a provincial capital lies just over the hill.

Quidi Vidi Battery

Quidi Vidi Battery (Cuckhold's Cove Rd., 709/729-2977; mid-May-Sept. daily 10am-5:30pm; adult $3) sits high on a hill above Quidi Vidi, overlooking the lake and village. The site owes its origin to the French, who built the battery in their effort to capture St. John's in 1762. France lost, and the British took the battery and rebuilt it in 1780. The site has been restored to its War of 1812 glory years, when England fortified the battery in anticipation of an attack by the United States that never materialized. The battery is now staffed by guides dressed in period uniforms of the Royal Artillery.

SOUTH OF DOWNTOWN
Bowring Park

Arguably the city's prettiest, Bowring Park has hosted significant guests for many tree-planting ceremonies, including a visit from Queen Elizabeth for the Cabot celebrations in 1997. Crocus and hyacinth beds make a colorful impact during spring, swans glide across the tranquil ponds in summer, and the setting is transformed into a canvas of dappled oranges and reds during autumn. Statues are everywhere, the most famous being of Peter Pan. It's a replica of the original in England's Kensington Gardens, and it serves as a memorial to Sir Edgar Bowring's godchild, who died in an offshore shipwreck.

To get there, stay south on Water Street until the road splits into Waterford Bridge and Topsail Roads; continue on Waterford Bridge Road for three kilometers to the park's entrance.

SIGHTS

ST. JOHN'S AND THE AVALON PENINSULA

Quidi Vidi

Cape Spear
National Historic Site

The eminently photogenic Cape Spear National Historic Site lighthouse (off Rte. 11, 709/772-5367; mid-May-mid-June Wed.-Sun. 10am-6pm, mid-June-early Sept. daily 10am-6pm, early Sept.-mid-Oct. Sat.-Wed. 9am-5pm; adult $4, senior $3.50, child $2) crowns a windy 75-meter-high promontory above the Atlantic Ocean. Built in 1839, the lighthouse ranks as the province's oldest extant beacon and was used until 1955, when the original lighting apparatus was moved to a more efficient building nearby. The keeper's living quarters have been restored, while the adjacent visitors center displays antiques and maritime artifacts.

Outside the lighthouse, the precipitous slopes hold the rusting remains of World War II gun batteries. Hiking trails fan out from the peak. The 10-kilometer trail to Maddox Cove starts here and winds south along the coast, through gullies, bakeapple bogs, and berry patches. If you're lucky, you'll see a family of shy foxes in the high grasses.

The cape, North America's most easterly point, lies six kilometers southeast of St. John's Harbour as the crow flies and 15 kilometers around Route 11's coastal curve. To get there, follow Water Street to the exit for Pitts Memorial Parkway and turn left to Route 11 (Blackhead Road).

PIPPY PARK

Civilization ends and wilderness begins at the Pippy Park preserve, which covers 1,343 hectares of woodlands, grasslands, and rolling hills on the steep hilltop plateau overlooking St. John's. In addition to the Fluvarium and the botanical garden, the park is laced with hiking trails and is home to two golf courses. Developed along the rim of the hill, the park fronts Confederation Parkway/Prince Philip Drive and encompasses Memorial University's campus and the government Confederation Building complex. Barrens, marshes, woodlands, ponds, and streams make for a splendid landscape. Moose, muskrat, mink, snowshoe hare, meadow voles, and common shrews roam the hilly terrain, which is studded with balsam fir, spruce, and juniper. The green-winged teal, black and pintail duck, sora rail, American bittern, gyrfalcon, and pied-billed grebe are among the birds lured to Long Pond, the oval lake near the park's edge. Long Pond marks the start of the seven-kilometer Rennies River Trail across the city's hillside to Quidi Vidi Lake.

Fluvarium

The eco-attraction Fluvarium (5 Nagle's Pl., 709/754-3474; July-Aug. Mon.-Fri. 9am-5pm, Sat.-Sun. 10am-5pm, Sept.-June Mon.-Fri. 9am-4:30pm, Sat.-Sun. noon-4:30pm; adult $7, senior $5, child $4) overlooks Long Pond from just north of Prince Philip Drive. It's contained in a handsome eight-sided wooden building wrapped with an open porch; you enter on the second floor, a spacious room with ecological exhibits depicting Atlantic salmon and other fish species, marsh birds, and carnivorous plants. The center's pièce de résistance is down a winding stairway. Nine windows pierce the walls and provide spectators a below-water-level look at the brook and brown trout, arctic char, and salmon in Nagle's Hill Brook. It's an innovative variation on the traditional aquarium.

Memorial University
Botanical Garden

The 38-hectare Memorial University Botanical Garden (306 Mt. Scio Rd., 709/737-8590; May-Aug. daily 10am-5pm, Sept.-Nov. daily 10am-4pm; adult $7, senior $5, child $3) is the province's only botanical garden. Garden environments include heather beds, a cottage garden, a rock garden, and a wildflower garden. Hiking trails wind through a boreal forest and a fen, both resplendent with native flowers, shrubs, and trees. The gardens feature a medley of soft colors. Blue forget-me-not, white turtlehead and rhododendron, and pink joe-pye weed bloom among spirea, northern wild raisin, dogwood, and high-bush cranberry. White birch, chokecherry, trembling aspen, ash, willow, and maple surround the botanical medley. To get to the gardens, follow Allandale Road north past Prince Philip Drive and turn west on Mt. Scio Road.

WEST OF DOWNTOWN
Bell Island

One of many islands in Conception Bay, west of St. John's, nine-kilometer-long Bell Island has a long history of mining. No. 2 Mine (709/488-2880; June-Sept. 10am-6pm; adult $12, senior $10, child $5), which stopped operating in 1949, remains one of the world's most productive submarine (underground) iron ore mines. The striking black-and-white photography of Yousuf Karsh is a highlight of the aboveground museum, while underground the main shaft has been restored and is open for inspection. Guided tours include the use of a hard hat, but you should bring your own sweater.

Newfoundlanders boast an incredible flair for artistic expression, an ability displayed in the Bell Island murals. Large-scale scenes painted on the sides of buildings depict the community's life and people during the ore-mining decades. Look for the half-dozen murals in different locations across the tiny island's northeastern corner, mainly in and near Wabana, the largest settlement. One assumes the murals were painted from historical photographs, yet there's a sense of real life to each painting—from a car's black luster to the animated figures and even the clear gleam of a miner's eyes.

To get to Bell Island, follow Route 40 west to Portugal Cove, 15 kilometers from downtown. The ferry (709/895-6931) operates year-round. In summer, sailings are every 20-40 minutes 7am-11:30pm. The fare is $9 per vehicle and driver, plus $4.50 per additional passenger.

TOURS
Sightseeing Tours

McCarthy's Party (709/579-4444, www.mccarthysparty.com) has been on the sightseeing tour scene for decades. From June to August the company offers daily 2.5-hour guided tours to Signal Hill, the cathedrals, and other major sites.

Walking Tours

One of many informal walking tours of downtown St. John's is Boyle's Walking Tours (709/364-6845, www.boyletours.com; mid-June-mid-Sept.), led by the very prim and proper Sir Cavendish Boyle. The Where They Once Stood tour ($20, cash only) departs Tuesday and Friday at 10am from the lobby of the Sheraton Hotel Newfoundland.

The Haunted Hike (709/685-3444, www.hauntedhike.com; June-mid-Sept.; $10) departs Sunday-Thursday at 9:30pm from the west entrance to the Anglican church at the corner of Duckworth Street and Church Hill. With the Reverend Thomas Wyckham Jarvis leading the way, you'll explore the darkened backstreets learning of murders, mysteries, and ghosts. It's an experience you won't forget in a hurry.

Recreation

Don't let bad weather prevent you from enjoying the outdoors—the locals certainly don't. Sure, it may be foggy or raining, but in many ways this adds to the St. John's experience when you're out hiking or striding the local fairways.

HIKING AND BIKING

The hilly streets of downtown St. John's aren't conducive to walking and biking, but if you're looking for wilderness, you don't need to travel too far from the city. A five-minute drive from downtown is Pippy Park. Follow Allendale Road north over the TransCanada Highway and look for the parking area beyond the golf course entrance. From this point, hiking trails loop past numerous lakes and through native forest.

Alongside the TransCanada Highway, 36 kilometers south of downtown, is Butter Pot Provincial Park, a 2,800-hectare wilderness of forests, bogs, and barrens—a taste of the interior a 30-minute drive from the city. The name "Butter Pot" is a local term for a rounded hill, many of which occur within the park boundary, including along Butter Pot Hill Trail, a 3.3-kilometer walk to a 300-meter-high summit. Along the way you'll see signs of ancient glacial action, including displaced boulders known as "erratics," while at the summit, hikers are rewarded with views extending north to Bell Island. This trail starts beside Site 58 of the park campground. With minimal elevation gain, the Peter's Pond Trail parallels a small lake from the day-use area; you can turn around after one kilometer or continue to Butter Pot Hill. A day pass is $5 per vehicle.

SCUBA DIVING

Situated on Atlantic Canada's oldest shipping routes, the St. John's area is incredibly rich in shipwrecks. What's more, the waters here are as clear as the Caribbean—20- to 30-meter visibility is common—and reasonably warm from summer to autumn, although a wetsuit is advisable. One of the most accessible wreck-diving sites is Lance Cove, on Bell Island, where four iron-ore carriers were torpedoed by German U-boats during World War II. Also in Conception Bay are much older whaling boats and a number of wrecks close enough to be accessible for shore diving. Based at Conception Bay South, Ocean Quest (17 Stanley's Rd., 709/834-7234, www.oceanquestadventures.com) takes divers to the bay and other dive sites for a full-day boat charter rate of $245 per person (includes rental gear). This company also operates a dive school, a dive shop, and a lodge.

Entertainment and Events

NIGHTLIFE

It's said St. John's has more pubs, taverns, and bars per capita than anyplace else in Atlantic Canada. Spend any time wandering through downtown after dark, and you'll probably agree. The city's international port status is partly the reason. Even better, these watering holes serve double duty as venues for music of various styles, including traditional Newfoundland, folk, Irish, country, rock, and jazz. The website www.georgestreetlive.ca has entertainment listings.

A local band of note is Great Big Sea, which combines modern rock and traditional Newfoundland folk to create a sound and atmosphere that draws sellout crowds throughout Canada.

"Screeched In"

Newfoundlanders dote on the codfish, and visitors are invited to pledge piscatorial loyalty to King Cod in hilarious induction ceremonies conducted on tours and in touristy restaurants. The tradition dates to the early 1900s, when a visiting U.S. naval officer followed the lead of his St. John's host by downing a glass of rum in one gulp. His reaction to swallowing the unlabeled rum was a undignified screech. And so the tradition was born, as U.S. servicemen docked in St. John's came ashore to sample the "screech."

To be "screeched in" in proper style, a visitor dons fishing garb, downs several quick shots of Screech rum, kisses a cod, joins in singing a local ditty, poses for a photograph, and receives an official certificate. It's strictly tourist nonsense, but visitors love it. Mostly because of its authentic atmosphere, Trapper John's (2 George St., 709/579-9630; daily noon-3am) in downtown St. John's is one of the best places to be "screeched in."

Pubs

The energetic pub scene centers on a one-block stretch of George Street off Water Street. The weekend starts late Friday evening, picks up again on Saturday afternoon, and lasts until 2am (and at some places keeps up through Sunday).

Among George Street's abundance of pubs and eating establishments, Trapper John's (2 George St., 709/579-9630; daily noon-3am) ranks as a city entertainment mainstay, hosting notable provincial folk groups and bands. The patrons will gladly initiate visitors to Newfoundland with a "screech-in" ceremony for free. Green Sleeves Pub (14 George St., 709/579-1070; daily 11am-close) doubles as a weekend hub for traditional, rock, and Irish concerts and jam sessions. Fat Cat Blues Bar (5 George St., 709/739-5554; Tues.-Sun. 8pm-3am) presents concerts, open mic, blues rock, and women's jam sessions.

Escape the frat-house atmosphere of George Street by pulling up a barstool at one of the cozy pubs dotted through surrounding downtown streets. Although it doesn't look like much from the outside, Erin's Pub (186 Water St., 709/722-1916; daily noon-3am) is a friendly place renowned for Celtic and local artists performing nightly except Sunday. Across the road, Nautical Nellies (201 Water St., 709/738-1120; daily 11am-3am) lives up to its name with decorations such as a scale model of the *Titanic* and cabinets filled with knotted rope. It's one of the most popular spots off George Street, so expect a crowd, especially on weekends.

The Ship Pub (265 Duckworth St., 709/753-3870; daily noon-2am) is a dimly lit room that has been a venue for local and provincial recording acts for years, and it continues to draw Newfoundland's hottest up-and-coming jazz, blues, and folk musicians each weekend night. These same artists, as well as literary types, are the main customers—you just never know who might be on stage or in the audience.

In the vicinity of the Ship Inn, the Crow's Nest (709/753-6927; Tues.-Thurs. 4:30-7:30pm, Fri. noon-10pm, Sat. 2pm-8pm) opened in 1942 as a retreat for naval officers, but this once-exclusive club is now open to interested visitors (dress code is "smart casual"). The old-fashioned room is a treasure trove of naval memorabilia, which includes a periscope from a German U-boat that was captured off St. John's during World War II. The club is on the fourth floor of an old brick warehouse between Water and Duckworth Streets; the entrance is opposite the war memorial.

PERFORMING ARTS

The Resource Centre for the Arts (LSPU Hall, 3 Victoria St., 709/753-4531, www.rca. nf.ca) stages productions by the resident RCA Theatre Company and also hosts professional touring groups throughout the year. Ticket prices vary depending on the event, but are always reasonable.

The Arts and Culture Centre (corner of Allandale Rd. and Prince Philip Dr., 709/729-3900) presents a wide range of theater, music, and dance on its Main Stage, with artists and troupes from across Canada. The center is also home to the Newfoundland Symphony Orchestra (709/722-4441, www.nsomusic.ca), which has a September-April season.

FESTIVALS AND EVENTS
Spring

The city shines as a music festival venue. The biggest and best is June's nine-day Festival 500 (709/738-6013, www.festival500.com), held in odd-numbered years. Highlights include the noontime medley of harbor ship horns; citywide theater, workshops, and dance; and Newfoundland, folk, electronic, jazz, New Age, and African concerts.

Summer

St. John's shares a Shakespeare by the Sea Festival (www.shakespearebytheseafestival.com) with Los Angeles and Sydney, Australia. The Newfoundland version takes place for three weeks in July, Friday-Sunday at 6pm. Expect outdoor productions of the Bard's best by the acclaimed Loyal Shakespearean Company. The venues change annually, but may be as dramatic as Cape Spear National Historic Site and as intimate as the Newman Wine Vault.

The Signal Hill Tattoo is a tribute to the landmark Battle of Signal Hill that ended the war between the English and French in North America. The military event is staged dramatically, with military drills by foot soldiers, artillery detachments, fife and drum bands, and more. It all takes place up at Signal Hill National Historic Site early July-mid-August on Wednesday, Thursday, Saturday, and Sunday at 11am and 3pm.

Beginning in late July or early August, Prince Edward Plaza on George Street is the outdoor setting for the weeklong George Street Festival (www.georgestreetlive.ca), which offers performances by top entertainers.

The Royal St. John's Regatta (709/576-8921, www.stjohnsregatta.org) is a city tradition that officially dates back to 1818 (making it North America's oldest organized sporting event), although it was probably contested as early as the late 1700s. What began as a rowing contest between visiting sailors has morphed into a world-class event drawing rowers from around the world. Held at Quidi Vidi Lake on the first Wednesday in August, the event draws up to 50,000 spectators and is so popular that the city long ago declared the day a civic holiday.

Winter

Most of the winter action centers on Mile One Centre (50 New Gower St., 709/576-7657, www.mileonecentre.com), where the St. John's IceCaps hockey franchise competes in the American Hockey League.

Shopping

An abundance of arts and crafts stores can be found in downtown St. John's. Aside from these, east along Duckworth Street beyond downtown is a string of interesting shops specializing in Newfoundland music, pet paraphernalia, and the like. My favorite is Johnny Ruth (181 Water St., 709/722-7477; Mon.-Wed. 10am-6pm, Thurs.-Fri. 10am-9pm, Sat. 10am-6pm, Sun. noon-5pm), which stocks locally printed shirts by Living Planet that feature a politically incorrect Newfoundland slant.

ARTS AND CRAFTS

Crafts shops downtown offer every conceivable craft available, and new developments continually increase the variety. One of the best places to start is Devon House (59 Duckworth St., 709/753-2749), in a historic building below the Sheraton Newfoundland. An outlet for the Craft Council of Newfoundland and Labrador, it displays an excellent sampling of traditional and contemporary wares.

For designer pieces, check out retail sales outlets in the artists' studios, such as Woof Design (181 Water St., 709/722-7555; summer daily 9am-5:30pm), which specializes in mohair, woolen, and angora apparel, plus whalebone carvings and other crafts. Other shops operate as cottage-industry outlets. Nonia Handicrafts (286 Water St., 709/753-8062; May-Dec. daily 10am-5:30pm, Jan.-April Tues.-Sat. 10am-5:30pm) is among the best crafts shops, carrying handwoven apparel, weavings, parkas, jewelry, hooked mats, domestic wares, and handmade toys.

Other shops sell a variety of wares: Grenfell parkas from St. Anthony, books about Newfoundland, local Purity-brand candies, tinned biscuits or seafood, bottles of savory spice, pottery and porcelain, handmade copper and tin kettles, model ships, soapstone and stone carvings, fur pelts and rugs, apparel, folk art, and handwoven silk, wool, cotton, and linen. Expect to find most of these goods at the Downhome Shoppe & Gallery (303 Water St., 709/722-2970; Mon.-Sat. 10am-5:30pm, Sun. noon-5:30pm).

Top-notch private galleries are plentiful. Christina Parker Gallery (50 Water St., 709/753-0580; Mon.-Fri. 10am-5:30pm, Sat. 11am-5:30pm) showcases Newfoundland's avant-garde spectrum; for more traditional art, plan on visiting the Emma Butler Gallery (111 George St., 709/739-7111; Tues.-Sat. 11am-5pm).

OUTDOOR GEAR

The Outfitters (220 Water St., 709/579-4453; Mon.-Sat. 10am-6pm, Sun. noon-5pm) sells an excellent range of outdoor wear, including winter jackets. It also has canoes, kayaks, and skis, and is a clearinghouse for information about outdoor recreation around the island.

Accommodations and Camping

While St. John's may not have a huge selection of budget accommodations, it does provide an excellent choice of historic B&Bs that offer excellent value. A few major chains are represented downtown (and are also well-priced), while you find all the familiar chains along major arteries. As elsewhere in Atlantic Canada, demand for rooms is highest in summer, and you should make reservations far in advance. While the larger downtown properties supply parking, at smaller properties you may be expected to use metered street parking.

DOWNTOWN
Under $50

Ensconced in one of the city's famously photogenic pastel-colored townhouses is HI-St. John's (8 Gower St., 709/754-4789, www.hihostels.ca), an affiliate of Hostelling International. Within walking distance of downtown, dorm rooms are spacious and come with a maximum of four beds. Other facilities include a well-equipped kitchen, a small backyard with a barbeque, and wireless Internet. Rates are $28 for members and $33 nonmembers. The double rooms are $75-85 and $85-89, respectively.

$50-100

Opposite Bannerman Park, Elizabeth Manor (21 Military Rd., 709/753-7733 or 888/263-3786, www.elizabethmanor.nl.ca; $80-199 s or d) was built in 1894, following the Great Fire of 1892. Completely revamped in 2004, it now offers four spacious en suite guest rooms, a sundeck, and a library with art and books about the province. Rates include a full breakfast.

$100-150

Waterford Manor (185 Waterford Bridge Rd., 709/754-4139, www.thewaterfordmanor.com; $125-265 s or d), a beautiful Queen Anne-style mansion near Bowring Park, is furnished with antiques of the late 19th century. The seven guest rooms vary greatly in size, but all have TVs and en suite bathrooms.

A restored Queen Anne-style townhouse, the Balmoral House (38 Queen's Rd., 709/754-5721 or 877/428-1055, www.balmoralhouse.com; $129-169 s or d) offers four large guest rooms, each with a fireplace, private bath, antique furnishings, TV, Internet access, and an expansive view of the harbor. Rates include a full breakfast and use of off-street parking.

Compton House (26 Waterford Bridge Rd., 709/722-0387, www.comptonhouse.travel; $129-249 s or d) once served as the mansion of C. A. Pippy, the merchant who donated St. John's local hilltop to the city for a park. The house has been grandly restored. Each of the 11 guest rooms has a private bath, and two have a whirlpool and fireplace or a full kitchen. Located south of downtown, it is a little longer walk to the harbor than from those B&Bs in the vicinity of Military Road, but there are no hills to negotiate.

Backing onto Bannerman Park and with a beautiful rear garden, ★ Banberry House (116 Military Rd., 709/579-8006 or 877/579-8226, www.banberryhouse.com; $139-169 s or d) oozes style throughout. My favorite of six guest rooms is the Labrador Room, which is filled with stylish mahogany furniture (including a work desk) and has a super-comfortable bed, a four-piece bath, and garden views. Rates include a full Newfoundland breakfast.

If you're traveling with children and want to stay downtown, Quality

Hotel-Harbourview (2 Hill O'Chips, 709/754-7788 or 800/228-5151, www.stjohnsqualityhotel.com; from $145 s or d) is a good choice. It has 162 midsized rooms, a popular restaurant overlooking the harbor, free outdoor parking, and free local calls. Rooms with harbor views start at $165, but check online for deals.

$150-200

In a graciously restored 1905 Queen Anne mansion across from Bannerman Park, Winterholme Suites & Spa (79 Rennies Mill Rd., 709/739-7979 or 800/599-7829, www.winterholme.com; $159-259 s or d) offers eight guest rooms, each with bold color schemes, jetted tubs, and TV/DVD combos.

Take a break from the city's abundant historic accommodations by reserving one of the spacious rooms at ★ Hometel on Signal Hill (10 St. Joseph's Lane, 709/739-7799 or 866/739-7799, www.hometels.ca; $160-210 s or d). Located near the base of Signal Hill but still an easy stroll to downtown, this newer lodging fills a row of modern townhouses, each containing up to eight guest rooms. The styling is contemporary throughout, with comfortable beds and large bathrooms adding to the appeal. A light breakfast is included in the rates, with guests congregating in a dining room above the lobby to fill themselves with toast, cereal, and fresh muffins.

Instead of a hotel with a restaurant, Blue on Water (319 Water St., 709/754-2583 or 877/431-2583, www.blueonwater.com; from $179 s or d) is a restaurant with 12 upstairs rooms. Like the Hometel on Signal Hill, it offers a modern ambience, but it is more centrally located. The decor is slick and contemporary—think 400-thread-count sheets, high-speed Internet connections, and flat-screen TVs. On the downside, the nearest parking is a public lot behind the property, there is no elevator, and check-in is within the restaurant. But once you're in your room, you'll think you're paying a lot more than you really are.

Hometel on Signal Hill

Across the road from the heart of the downtown waterfront, a row of 1846 wooden warehouses has been transformed into **Murray Premises Hotel** (5 Becks Cove, 709/738-7773 or 866/738-7773, www.murraypremiseshotel.com; $189-249 s or d). The 67 rooms fill the top two floors and an adjacent wing. Each is super-spacious and features luxurious touches such as maple furniture, heated towel racks and jetted tubs in the oversized bathrooms, and TV/DVD combos. In-room coffee, complimentary newspapers, and free wireless Internet add to the appeal.

Closer to the airport than to the waterfront, the **Holiday Inn St. John's** (180 Portugal Cove Rd., 709/722-0506 or 800/933-0506, www.ihg.com; $165 s or d) is handy to Pippy Park, Memorial University, and the Confederation Building complex. The 256 guest rooms were last revamped in 2004; other amenities include indoor and outdoor pools and a restaurant, lounge, laundry, business center, hairdresser, and shopping arcade.

Outside of the summer season, check online for rooms around $120.

Over $200

Sheraton Hotel Newfoundland (115 Cavendish Sq., 709/726-4980 or 800/325-3535, www.starwoodhotels.com; from $240 s or d) has an auspicious location, on the former site of Fort William. The first Hotel Newfoundland, one of Canadian Pacific's deluxe properties, opened in 1925. After many years' service, it was demolished to make room for this handsome hotel. Opened in 1982, the hillside property has more than 300 guest rooms, free parking, and a contemporary restaurant, lounge, fitness center (with an indoor pool, table tennis, squash courts, sauna, and whirlpool), and shopping arcade with a hairdresser.

Delta St. John's (120 New Gower St., 709/739-6404 or 888/890-3222, www.deltahotels.com; from $240 s or d) is an avant-garde high-rise that offers more than 400 rooms and suites; restaurants and a pub; fitness facilities that include an indoor heated pool, exercise equipment, whirlpool, sauna, and squash courts; a shopping arcade; and covered parking.

AIRPORT
$100-150

Comfort Inn Airport (106 Airport Rd., 709/753-3500, www.comfortinnstjohns.com; $129-149 s or d) is conveniently located across from St. John's International Airport and features 100 rooms and suites, a restaurant and lounge, a business center, a fitness center, airport transfers, and free continental breakfast.

CONCEPTION BAY
$100-150

★ **Ocean Quest Adventure Resort** (17 Stanley's Rd., Conception Bay South, 709/834-7234 or 866/623-2664, www.oceanquestcharters.com; $109 s, $129-149 d) is a purpose-built accommodation that revolves around divers and their needs, but everyone is welcome. The rooms feature clean contemporary layouts, and one has a jetted tub. The downstairs common area has a library of books, a TV where you can watch dive videos, a kitchen, and a deck with a propane barbecue. Attached to the accommodation is a dive shop and dive school with an indoor heated pool. Rates include breakfast, but many guests stay as part of a package that includes diving.

CAMPGROUNDS

Pippy Park Campground (Nagle's Pl., 709/737-3669, www.pippypark.com; May-Sept.; $24-45), 2.5 kilometers northwest of downtown, fills on a first-come, first-served basis. It offers more than 150 sites, most of which are private and well spaced. Amenities include a general store, a playground, wireless Internet (in only one section of the campground), and picnic shelters. The Fluvarium (great for children) is across the road, while

trails lead from the campground to all corners of Pippy Park.

Butter Pot Provincial Park, along the TransCanada Highway, 36 kilometers south of downtown, has a 126-site campground. The cost is $23 per night, with showers and laundry facilities provided. Each private site has a fire pit and picnic table. Activities include hiking and water sports such as lake swimming and canoeing (rentals available). Three playgrounds will keep the young ones occupied.

Farther out, but in a beautiful lakeside location, ★ **La Manche Provincial Park** (Rte. 10; late May-late Sept.; $15-23) has 83 campsites spread around two forested loops. Although there are no showers or hookups, the facility fills every summer weekend. In addition to kayaking and fishing, campers take advantage of trails leading along La Manche River and down to an abandoned fishing village.

Food

No one would describe the St. John's dining scene as sophisticated, but it is better—by far—than anywhere else in the province. As you might imagine, seafood features prominently on most menus. Cod is a staple, while in better restaurants you find Atlantic salmon, mussels, scallops, halibut, and lobster.

CAFÉS AND CHEAP EATS

The ★ **Bagel Café** (246 Duckworth St., 709/739-4470; Mon.-Wed. 7am-9pm, Thurs.-Sun. 7am-10pm; lunches $7-11) feels more like a restaurant than a coffeehouse. All breakfasts are under $10, including heart-smart options like poached eggs and cereal with low-fat yogurt. Potato bakes make a tasty treat, or order something more substantial, like lasagna.

If you're looking for good, locally roasted coffee in a modern city-style setting, stop by **Hava Java** (258 Water St., 709/753-5282; Mon.-Wed. 7:30am-6pm, Thurs.-Fri.

7:30am-9pm, Sat. 8am-9pm, Sun. 8am-6pm; lunches $7-10), which is in the heart of busy Water Street. Food offerings are the usual soup and sandwiches.

Jumping Bean (47 Harvey Rd., 709/754-4538; Mon.-Fri. 7:30am-6pm, 9am-5pm, Sun. 10am-4pm; lunches $7-11) is a quiet place away from the downtown core. The owners are primarily coffee-roasters, so you know you'll be getting the very freshest coffee, but you can also try the most unique flavor in the province—Screech Coffee, which is infused with Newfoundland rum.

DELIS

Along downtown's busiest street, ★ **Rocket** (272 Water St., 709/738-2011; Mon.-Fri. 7:30am-9pm, Sat. 8am-10pm, Sun. 8am-6pm; lunches $7-12) is a deli with a difference. It stocks all the goodies you would expect to find in a Newfoundland deli, as well as bakery and lunch items, soups and sandwiches, and a huge selection of teas and coffees. Many customers pick up their orders and move on to the adjacent room, which is not really a restaurant but somewhere to simply sit down and eat lunch.

The lower end of Freshwater Road has a concentration of bakeries and delicatessens. **Stockwood's Bakery and Delicatessen** (316 Freshwater Rd., 709/726-2083; 24 hours daily) stocks fresh sandwiches, cold plates, salads, cakes, and baking supplies, and is never closed. For a selection of fancier cakes and pastries, stop by **Manna European Bakery & Deli** (342 Freshwater Rd., 709/739-6992; daily 7am-7pm).

Head to the **Seafood Shop** (7 Rowan St., Churchill Sq., 709/753-1153; Mon.-Sat. from 8am) for fresh and packaged seafood such as cod, shrimp, halibut, mussels, and scallops.

For a tantalizing overview of Newfoundland cuisine, head to ★ **Bidgoods** (Rte. 10, Goulds, 709/368-3125; Mon.-Sat. 9am-7pm, Sun. 10am-6pm), on the south side of the city. This 50-year-old store stocks every taste sensation known to the province, including seal flipper pie, caribou, salted fish, salmon, and cod tongues and cheeks. Not much is prepackaged here, but the produce (especially west coast strawberries), berry preserves, shellfish, smoked and pickled fish, and sweet tea biscuits make delicious picnic additions.

PUB GRUB

★ **Nautical Nellies** (201 Water St., 709/738-1120; food service Sun.-Thurs. 5pm-9pm; $12-16) has some of the best pub grub in town, but it doesn't serve food during the busy weekend evenings. The rest of the week, enjoy a pile of steamed mussels, crab spring rolls with jalapeño dipping sauce, pan-fried cod with a side of scrunchions (tiny pieces of fried pork fat), or British dishes like steak and kidney pie.

The **Ship Pub** (265 Duckworth St., 709/753-3870; food service daily noon-3pm; lunches $7.50-13) is a cozy neighborhood pub best known for its live music, but you can order simple lunches from the inexpensive blackboard menu.

REGIONAL CUISINE

"Newfoundland cuisine" revolves around seafood, and traditionally, it's been deep-fried, which is often bemoaned by outsiders not used

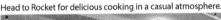
Head to Rocket for delicious cooking in a casual atmosphere.

to this style of cooking. That said, it's worth trying fish-and-chips at least once—and not at a regular family restaurant, but somewhere it is a specialty, such as Ches's Fish and Chips (9 Freshwater Rd., 709/722-4083; $9-16). Here, tender deep-fried fillets and crisp french fries are served in an atmosphere of Formica and bright lights.

Walk a few blocks east of downtown to reach Classic Café East (73 Duckworth St., 709/579-4444; daily 8am-9pm; $13-21), a popular spot that gets crowded with all types who come seeking delicious seafood chowder, cod tongues with scrunchions, and other traditional Newfoundland fare at moderate prices in a cozy atmosphere. For desert, try the spotted dick (a traditional steamed pudding) or the cheesecake with partridgeberry sauce.

A huge step up in style and price, but still rooted in traditional cooking, is Bacalao (65 Lemarchant Rd., 709/579-6565; Mon. 6pm-10pm, Tues.-Fri. noon-2:30pm and 6pm-10pm, Sat.-Sun.11am-2:30pm and 6pm-10pm; $18-33), which means "salt cod" in Spanish. Within a stylish setting, top chefs serve up Newfoundland's best known export, cod, in a number of creative ways, using local, organic ingredients whenever possible. The local theme extends through many dishes—mussels are steamed open in Quidi Vidi beer, and the caribou salad is drizzled with blueberry wine from the province's only winery. As an entrée, the salted cod poached in olive oil and accompanied by smoked and braised pork belly is hard to fault, or choose dishes such as seafood risotto and Game of the Day (it was caribou with partridgeberry sauce last time I visited). Save room for a slice of patriotic Republic Mousse, which is decorated in the three colors of the Newfoundland flag.

CONTEMPORARY

The chic industrial-style signage out front is a giveaway—Magnum & Steins (329 Duckworth St., 709/576-6500; Sun.-Thurs. 5:30pm-10pm, Fri.-Sat. 5:30pm-11pm; $28-45) is clearly unlike any other restaurant in the city. If you're looking for a traditional Newfoundland experience, eat elsewhere. If you're looking for creative city-style cooking and top-notch presentation, this place is a welcome break from deep-fried seafood.

Blue on Water (319 Water St., 709/754-2583; daily for breakfast, lunch, and dinner; $29-46) is a smallish modern space with a bright atmosphere. Modern cooking is combined with traditional foods in dishes such as kippered mackerel baked with cream and shallots. Lunches include gourmet sandwiches and a delicious seafood bouillabaisse. In the evening, things get serious (and expensive) with starters like shrimp in a coconut tempura and spicy pineapple chutney and mains like salmon stuffed with roasted red peppers and spinach. The wine list covers all bases.

East Indian

Fine East Indian cuisine can be found at India Gate (286 Duckworth St., 709/753-6006; Mon.-Fri. 11:30am-2pm, daily 5pm-10pm; $12-20). The extensive menu includes tandoori dishes; prawns, lamb, beef, and chicken cooked in the masala, korma, and vindaloo styles; and a wide array of vegetarian entrées. Prices are inexpensive to moderate, portions are generous, and the atmosphere is quiet and relaxed.

Information and Services

Tourist Information

The provincial tourism office (709/729-2830 or 800/563-6353, www.newfoundlandlabrador.com) and Destination St. John's (709/739-8899 or 877/739-8899, www.destinationstjohns.com) are both good sources of information when planning your trip.

There's an information booth at the

airport (open whenever flights are arriving) and another just beyond the ferry dock at Argentia (open for all ferry arrivals). When you get downtown, search out the City of St. John's Visitor Information Centre (348 Water St., 709/576-8106, www.stjohns.ca; May-early Oct. daily 9am-4:30pm, early Oct.-April Mon.-Fri. 9am-4:30pm), in a three-story red-brick building by the Delta St. John's.

Health and Safety

Local hospitals under the jurisdiction of Eastern Health include the General Hospital (300 Prince Philip Dr., 709/737-6335), Janeway Children's Health Centre (also at 300 Prince Phillip Dr., 709/778-4228), and St. Clare's Mercy Hospital (154 LeMarchant Rd., 709/777-5501).

The Royal Newfoundland Constabulary (911 or 709/729-8333) deals with police matters within city limits, while the Royal Canadian Mounted Police (709/772-5400) protect the rest of the province.

Transportation

Even though St. John's sits on the far eastern edge of the North American continent, it is a transportation hub for air travel through the province and for shipping routes across the Atlantic Ocean.

GETTING THERE

Air

St. John's International Airport (www.st-johnsairport.com) is off Portugal Cove Road, a simple 15-minute drive northwest from downtown. The airport is a large modern facility, with ATMs, a currency exchange center, an information booth (open daily until the arrival of the last flight), a restaurant and lounge, a duty-free shop, a newsstand, and car-rental desks for all the major companies (Avis, Budget, Discount, Hertz, National, and Thrifty). Taxis charge a flat rate to any of the major downtown hotels: $28 for the first person, $6 each additional person.

St. John's is served by direct Air Canada (709/726-7880 or 888/247-2262) flights from Halifax, Montréal, and Toronto, with connections made through these three cities from its worldwide network. WestJet (888/937-8538) uses Halifax as its eastern hub, from where regular connections can be made to St. John's. Local airlines include Provincial Airlines (709/576-3943 or 800/563-2800, www.provincialairlines.com), with flights between Halifax and St. John's, plus onward flights throughout the province and Air Saint-Pierre (902/873-3566, www.airsaintpierre.com), with daily shuttle services to the St-Pierre and Miquelon Islands.

Car

If you are coming by car from the mainland, you need to get to Sydney, Nova Scotia. From here, two ferry routes cross to Newfoundland. The longer and more expensive option is to catch the ferry from Sydney to Argentia. Taking this route, you are left with a much shorter drive upon reaching Newfoundland. Downtown St. John's is 134 kilometers east of Argentia, via Route 100 and Route 1.

The alternative is to catch the ferry from Sydney to Port-aux-Basques, a short trip, but one that leaves you with a 900-kilometer (11-hour) drive across the province to St. John's via the TransCanada Highway.

From Halifax, it's 430 kilometers to Sydney, so allow around 22 hours, inclusive of either ferry crossing, to reach St. John's.

Ferry

One of two ferry services to Newfoundland from North Sydney (Nova Scotia) docks at Argentia, a 134-kilometer drive south of St. John's. Ferries are operated by Marine Atlantic (709/227-2431 or 800/341-7981, www.marine-atlantic.ca) two times weekly mid-June to late September (at other time of year, you will need to use the Sydney to Port-Aux-Basques route). The trip over from the mainland takes 14 hours and costs adult $115, senior $105, child $56, and from $233 for vehicles. Dorm beds and cabins are also available.

Bus

There is no bus service between the ferry terminal at Argentia and St. John's. For those arriving in Newfoundland via the ferry to Port-aux-Basques, DRL-LR (709/263-2171) operates long-haul bus service to St. John's (14 hours; $138 one-way).

GETTING AROUND

Locals complain that downtown parking space is scarce. Not so, the city says, countering that there are 1,500 parking slots at the Municipal Parking Garage on Water Street, other downtown garages, and on the streets. Some 800 street spaces are metered for loonies (the $1 coin) and quarters; when the time is up, the cops are quick to ticket expired meters.

Bus

Metrobus (709/570-2020, www.metrobus.

com) operates an extensive bus network that leads from downtown to all outer suburbs. Transfers are valid for 90 minutes of travel in one direction. The cost is adult $2.25, child $1.75 per sector.

Taxi

Cabs wait at the airport ($28 to downtown for one person, then $6 for each additional) and also out front of major hotels like the Delta St. John's and Sheraton Hotel Newfoundland. Travel within downtown runs $6-10. Major companies include City Wide (709/722-0003), Jiffy (709/722-2222), and Co-op (709/726-6666).

Car and RV Rental

All major rental car companies are represented in St. John's, but check local restrictions, such as bans on traveling to certain parts of the island and along the TransLabrador Highway.

Islander RV (709/738-7368 or 888/848-2267, www.islanderrv.com) charges $184 per day for a two-person camper and from $254 for an RV that sleeps six. Per day, 150 free kilometers are included, and there's a seven-day minimum rental during summer.

Avalon Peninsula

If sightseeing time is short and you must bypass the rest of Newfoundland, consider the Avalon Peninsula as a manageable stand-in. Although it is known by a single name, it is actually four peninsulas, two jutting southward and two northward. The city of St. John's sprawls across one. The highlights of the remaining three are covered in this section.

BACCALIEU TRAIL

This route hugs the northern Avalon coastline, winding around Conception Bay to the town of Carbonear and then looping south along the east side of Trinity Bay back to the TransCanada Highway. The loop makes an

ideal full-day trip from St. John's (around 380 kilometers), but accommodations en route may tempt you to stay longer.

Brigus

Picturesque Brigus lies across Conception Bay from Conception Bay South, or around 50 minutes' drive via the TransCanada Highway and Route 63. The town's most famous native son, Captain Robert Bartlett, was an Arctic explorer who accompanied Robert Peary on his 1908 North Pole expedition. Bartlett's 1820 house is now Hawthorne Cottage National Historic Site (corner of South St. and Irishtown Rd., 709/528-4004;

The home of Arctic explorer Robert Bartlett is now protected as Hawthorne Cottage National Historic Site.

mid-May-late June Wed.-Sun. 9:30am-5:30pm, late June-early Sept. daily 9am-6pm, early Sept.-early Oct. Wed.-Sun. 9:30am-5:30pm; adult $5, senior $4.50, child $3). Built in 1830, the cottage is a rare intact example of the *cottage orné* (decorative) style, with interpretive panels dotting the gardens telling the stories of Bartlett's northern exploits.

Numerous small town cafés dot the Baccalieu Trail, but none is more welcoming than **Country Corner** (14 Water St., 709/528-1099; May-Oct. daily 10am-6pm; lunches $5.50-9), where highlights include a bowl of steaming cod chowder, moose stew, and a selection of ice-cream desserts.

GETTING THERE

Brigus is 10 kilometers (10 minutes) north of Conception Harbour via Route 60 and about 85 kilometers (one hour) west of St. Johns, via Route 1 and Route 70.

Cupids

Plantation owner John Guy established Cuper's Cove in 1610, making what is now called Cupids the oldest British settlement in Canada. Artifacts can be seen at the worthwhile **Cupids Legacy Centre** (368 Seaforest Dr., 709/528-1610; mid-June-mid-Oct. daily 9:30am-5pm; adult $8.50, senior $7.60, child $4.25), with many modern, interactive displays. Down on the waterfront and within walking distance of the Legacy Centre is the **Plantation Site,** an ongoing dig that continues to unearth the remains of Guy's plantation. Visitors are welcome to view the dig on 20-minute guided tours. These leave on demand (book through the Legacy Centre; June-early Oct. daily 9am-4:30pm) and cost adult $6, senior $4, child $3.

GETTING THERE

Cupids is about three kilometers north of Brigus via Keatings Road.

Harbour Grace

Once the second-largest town in Newfoundland, Harbour Grace suffered a series of setbacks when seven fires besieged the town over the span of a century. Many of its oldest buildings survived and now make up the **Harbour Grace Heritage District.** Named "Havre de Grace" by the French in the early 16th century, the town boasts both pirates and pilots in its heritage. **Conception Bay Museum** (Water St., 709/596-5465; July-Aug. daily 10am-5pm; adult $2, child $1) occupies the former site of the lair of Peter Easton, a notorious pirate of the early 1600s. It's in a three-story red-brick building along the harbor front. Three centuries later, on May 20, 1932, Harbour Grace gained fame when Amelia Earhart took off from the local airfield to become the first woman to fly solo across the Atlantic. The grassed runway of Harbour Grace airfield is now a national historic site. To get there, follow Military Road from the main street through to the north side of town and take the signposted unpaved road under the highway to the top of the hill.

Before her famous flight, Amelia Earhart stayed at the red-brick **Hotel Harbour Grace** (66 Water St., 709/596-5156, www. hotelharbourgrace.ca; $90-120 s or d), but a better option today is the **Rothesay House Inn** (34 Water St., 709/596-2268 or 877/596-2268, www.rothesay.com; $125-140 s or d), where the four guest rooms have a distinct Victorian-era look. Rates include a cooked breakfast; dinner is $38 per person by advance reservation.

GETTING THERE

To get to Harbour Grace from Brigus, you can take Route 75 (32 kilometers, 30 minutes) or Route 70 (28 kilometers, 30 minutes) north. From St. John's, it's about 110 kilometers (1.5 hours) west and north along Route 1 and Route 70 to Harbour Grace.

Grates Cove

The peninsula's northernmost village, Grates Cove retains the look and feel of Ireland perhaps more than any other Irish-settled community, thanks to the hundreds of rock walls erected as livestock and farm enclosures by early settlers.

Off the eastern end of the peninsula's tip,

the **Baccalieu Island Ecological Reserve** shelters 11 species of seabirds, including Leach's storm-petrels, black-legged kittiwakes, gannets, fulmars, and puffins.

GETTING THERE

To get to Grates Cove from Harbour Grace, it's a 75-kilometer (one hour) drive north on Route 70. From St. John's, it's about 180 kilometers (2.5 hours) to Grates Cove west along Route 1, then north on Route 75 and Route 70.

Heart's Content

The first successful transatlantic telegraph cables came ashore in 1866 at Heart's Content, 23 kilometers northwest of Carbonear. One of the original cables, which extended from Valentia Island on the west coast of Ireland, is still visible at the shoreline. Across the road, the restored **Heart's Content Cable Station** (Rte. 80, 709/583-2160; mid-May-early Oct. daily 9:30am-5pm; adult $6, senior $4, child $3) displays some of the original equipment.

GETTING THERE

To get to Heart's Content from Grates Cove, take Route 70 south, then take Route 80 south. It's a 60-kilometer (50-minute) drive. If you're driving directly to Heart's Content from St. John's, it's a 130-kilometer (1.5 hours) drive west along Route 1, then north along Route 75 and Route 74.

Dildo

Best known for its risqué name (thought to have been bestowed by Captain Cook in reference to a phallic offshore island), Dildo lies at the head of Trinity Bay, 12 kilometers north of the TransCanada Highway. The history of the 19th-century codfish hatchery on Dildo Island—the first commercial hatchery in Canada—is depicted at the **Dildo and Area Interpretation Centre** (Rte. 80, 709/582-2687; June-Sept. daily 10am-6pm; adult $2, child $1), along with a display of Dorset Inuit harpoon tips estimated to be 1,700 years old. Out front is a replica of an 8.5-meter-long squid pulled from local waters.

High above Trinity Bay, ★ **Inn by the Bay** (78 Front Rd., 709/582-3170 or 888/339-7829, www.dildoinns.com; $109-189 s or d) stacks up as equal to the best B&Bs in St. John's in all regards—with sweeping water views as a free extra. No stone has been left unturned in transforming this 1888 home into a seven-room inn, right down to supercomfortable beds topped with feather-filled duvets and striking antiques that fill the veranda sunroom. Rates include a full breakfast and afternoon tea; dinner in the sea-level dining room, which overlooks the bay, is highly recommended.

GETTING THERE

To get to Dildo from Heart's Content, drive south on Route 80 for 45 kilometers (40 minutes). To get to Dildo directly from St. John's, take Route 1 west, then Route 80 north, for a total of 100 kilometers (1.5 hours).

ST. JOHN'S TO FERRYLAND

From downtown St. John's, it's a little over 70 kilometers (one hour) to Ferryland, the ideal turnaround point for a day trip from the capital—except that there are a couple of stops en route worth as much time as you can afford.

★ Witless Bay Ecological Reserve

Newfoundland's seabird spectacle spreads across three offshore islands near the **Witless Bay Ecological Reserve**, 30 kilometers south of St. John's. Overwhelming displays of more than a million pairs of Atlantic puffins, Leach's storm-petrels, murres, black-legged kittiwakes, herring gulls, Atlantic razorbills, black guillemots, and black-backed and herring gulls are the attraction here. The season spans May-August and peaks from mid-June to mid-July. Whale numbers in local waters have increased dramatically in the last two decades, and this is mirrored in the number of operators running whale-watching trips. Between May and September, you are most likely to see humpbacks, but killer, fin, and minke whales are also present throughout the reserve. Seeing icebergs is also a possibility.

The closest tour operators to St. John's are **O'Brien's Whale and Bird Tours** (Lower Rd., 709/753-4850 or 877/639-4253; adult $58,

aboard one of O'Brien's Whale and Bird Tours

senior $52, child $40) and Gatherall's Puffin and Whale Watch (Northside Rd., 709/334-2887 or 800/419-4253), which are both based at Bay Bulls, 31 kilometers south. O'Brien's is a well-organized operation, complete with a choice of vessels and an onshore gift shop and restaurant. Pickups are available from any St. John's lodging (adult $25, child $20). The village of Bauline East, 15 kilometers south of Bay Bulls, is a lot closer to the birds and whales, meaning less time spent reaching the reserve. Here, Colbert's (709/334-3773) departs regularly from the local wharf on one-to two-hour trips for around $45 per person. You can make reservations, but during quieter times, boats leave on demand.

La Manche Provincial Park

La Manche Provincial Park was established in the 1960s to protect a scenic valley 53 kilometers south of St. John's along Route 10. The valley comes to an abrupt end at a cove surrounded by high cliffs, and here lies the most interesting aspect of the park. In 1840 a small village developed at the head of the cove, complete with a school, general store, and wooden "flakes" for drying fish. In 1966 a wild winter storm destroyed most of the settlement. The government resettled the residents, and today concrete foundations and a reconstructed suspension bridge are all that remains. To get there, drive down the fire road beyond the park campground; from the gate, it's 1.5 kilometers to the cove (allow one hour for the round-trip). The campground (late May-late Sept.; $15-23) has 69 campsites spread around two loops. There are no showers or hookups.

FERRYLAND

This east coast port, 70 kilometers south of St. John's, is one of Canada's oldest fishing villages, and the site of the colony founded by Sir George Calvert in 1621. To him, the region was akin to King Arthur's heavenly paradise, a haven for the beleaguered Roman Catholics from England. Or so he thought. Once settled at Ferryland, Calvert's colony endured diminishing supplies and harsh winters. His wife and son and a number of other colonists headed south to Maryland, and Calvert followed, leaving the plantation and the name of Avalon. Today, Ferryland is one of the most attractive communities on the Avalon Peninsula, but an archaeological dig in the heart of the community draws most visitors.

★ Colony of Avalon

An ongoing archaeological dig and a sparkling interpretive center combine to make the drive from St. John's worthwhile. The Colony of Avalon Interpretation Centre (709/432-3200; early June-early Oct. daily 10am-6pm; adult $11.50, senior $10, student $9) is a big two-story building where display panels tell of Ferryland's long history, with the help of hundreds of artifacts used by the original settlers. Upstairs is a laboratory where you can watch archaeologists at work documenting the finds. The herb garden out front replicates one from the era of the original Colony of Avalon.

From the interpretive center, it's a short walk through the modern-day village to the dig site, where you can watch archaeologists at work weekdays mid-June to mid-October. Admission to the interpretive center includes a 90-minute guided walk around the site, where you can see the remnants of a cobblestone street and the site of Calvert's mansion.

Shamrock Festival

The two-day Shamrock Festival (709/432-2052, www.ssfac.com) crowds the town on the last full weekend in July. Thousands of music fans gather within a roped-off area in the heart of the village (along with a few hundred on a distant hillside) to listen to some of Newfoundland's top musicians. The atmosphere is both welcoming and unforgettable—you'll find yourself surrounded by the lilt of Irish accents, the smells of an outdoor fair mixed with fresh ocean air, and the sounds of foot-stomping Celtic music. A plastic cup of Quidi Vidi beer rounds out the experience.

Food

Ferryland doesn't have a great deal of visitor

services, but as most visitors are day-trippers from the capital, this isn't a problem.

Earn your lunch by walking up to the headland, through town, to reach ★ **Lighthouse Picnics** (709/363-7456; mid-June-mid-Sept. Wed.-Sun. 11:30am-4:30pm), which operates out of the 1870 red-and-white lighthouse. Order food as simple as baked-daily muffins, or a full picnic lunch of gourmet cheeses, crab cakes, and strawberry shortcake. Picnic baskets—along with blankets—are supplied.

Getting There

Ferryland is about 70 kilometers (one hour) south of St. John's via Route 10.

CONTINUING ALONG THE IRISH LOOP

From Ferryland, Route 10 continues south for 58 kilometers, then heads west and north as Route 90 to St. Catherines. From this point, you can head south to Cape St. Mary's or north past Salmonier Nature Park back to the TransCanada Highway. This comprises the Irish Loop. While almost 50 percent of Newfoundlanders are of Irish descent, the strong accents and Celtic traditions are more prevalent here than elsewhere in the province.

Mistaken Point Ecological Reserve

At the southern end of the Avalon Peninsula, **Mistaken Point Ecological Reserve** lies alongside a remote coastline. To explore the area, turn off Route 10 at Portugal Cove South and follow the unmarked gravel road 16 kilometers to Long Beach, where the reserve's gently rolling headland stretches to the sea. Bring a warm jacket to fend off the strong winds, and be ready for thick fog banks from June to mid-July. Hikers enjoy the trails that meander across the reserve, and photographers relish the offshore boulders and turbulent surf. The rocks at the ecological reserve, acclaimed as one of Canada's most important fossil sites, contain impressions of 20 different species of multicellular marine creatures that lived 620 million years ago.

Salmonier Nature Park

Salmonier Nature Park, on Route 90 halfway between the TransCanada Highway and St. Catherines (709/229-7189; June-Aug. daily 10am-5pm, Sept. daily 10am-3pm; free) is well worth searching out. A two-kilometer

a guided tour through the Colony of Avalon

boardwalk and wood-chip trail runs through a sample forest and across bogs, which back up to the Avalon Wilderness Reserve. Moose, caribou, lynx, bald eagles, snowy owls, otters, beavers, mink, and other indigenous species are exhibited in natural-habitat enclosures.

CAPE SHORE

The Cape Shore juts into Placentia Bay west of the main body of the Avalon Peninsula. It's 215 kilometers from the TransCanada Highway, south through Salmonier to St. Bride's, and back to the TransCanada Highway, 33 kilometers west of the starting point. The highlight of the region is the bird colony at Cape St. Mary's.

Argentia

Argentia is the arrival point for ferries from Sydney, Nova Scotia. Formerly a U.S. naval base, the bay is now dominated by the ferry terminal, but trails lead to lookouts, abandoned bunkers, and good vantage points for watching local bird life.

Marine Atlantic ferries (709/227-2431 or 800/341-7981, www.marine-atlantic.ca) arrive at Argentia two times weekly during a mid-June to mid-October sailing season. One-way fares for the 14-hour sailing from North Sydney (Nova Scotia) are adult $115, senior $105, child $56, and from $233. Beyond the ferry terminal is Argentia Provincial Visitor Information Centre (709/227-5272), which opens in conjunction with ferry arrivals. From Argentia, drive south through Placentia to reach Cape St. Mary's or head northwest along Route 100 to the TransCanada Highway, which leads into downtown St. John's (allow 90 minutes from Argentia).

GETTING THERE
Argentia is 8 kilometers north of Placentia (via Charter Avenue) and 130 kilometers (1.5 hours) southwest of St. John's via Route 100 and the TransCanada Highway.

One of two ferry services to Newfoundland from North Sydney (Nova Scotia) docks at Argentia. Ferries are operated by Marine Atlantic (709/227-2431 or 800/341-7981, www.marine-atlantic.ca) two times weekly mid-June to late September (at other times of year, you will need to use the Sydney to Port-Aux-Basques route). The trip over from the mainland takes 14 hours and costs adult $115, senior $105, child $56, and from $233 for vehicles. Dorm beds and cabins are also available.

Placentia

France chose the magnificent coastal forest area overlooking Placentia Bay for its early island capital, Plaisance, and colonists and soldiers settled here in 1662. The early military fortification crowned a high hill overlooking the port at what is now Jerseyside. The French launched assaults on St. John's from Le Gaillardin, the first small fort of 1692, and then from Fort Royal, the massive stone fortress built the following year. England gained possession of the settlement in 1713 and renamed it Placentia. The hill on which the fortress stands became known as Castle Hill. Exhibits at the visitors center of Castle Hill National Historic Site (709/227-2401; June-Aug. daily 10am-6pm; adult $4, senior $3.50, child $2) document French and English history at Placentia. Guided tours are offered in summer. Picnic tables are available, and trails run along the peak's fortifications and the bay's stone beach.

GETTING THERE
Placentia is 130 kilometers southwest of St. John's, eight kilometers south of Argentia via Charter Avenue. Get there via the TransCanada Highway and Route 100.

★ Cape St. Mary's Ecological Reserve

The Cape St. Mary's Ecological Reserve lies at the Cape Shore's southern tip, 16 kilometers down an unpaved road off Route 100. If you're traveling down from St. John's, allow at least three hours; from the ferry terminal at Argentia, head south for 75 kilometers (allow at least an hour). At the end of the road is an **interpretive center** (709/277-1666; mid-May-early Oct. daily 9am-5pm; free). From this point, a one-kilometer trail leads across the steeply banked headland to North America's most accessible bird sanctuary. You'll hear the birds long before they come into view. And then all of a sudden, Bird Rock emerges in front of you—a 60-meter-high sea stack jammed with some 60,000 seabirds. The rocky pyramid seems to come alive with fluttering, soaring birds, whose noisy calls drift out to sea on the breezes. Expect to see northern gannets in one of North America's largest colonies (10,000 nesting pairs), common and thick-billed murres, and black-legged kittiwakes, along with some razorbills, black guillemots, great black-backed gulls, and herring gulls.

Warning: The trail is often slippery and comes very close to precipitous cliffs, so be very careful. Also, be prepared for bad weather by dressing warmly and in layers.

The closest accommodation to Cape St. Mary's is **Bird Island Resort** (Rte. 100, 709/337-2450 or 888/337-2450, www.birdislandresort.com; $85-130 s or d), in St. Bride's, 20 kilometers north. Overlooking Placentia Bay, the "resort" comprises five motel rooms, 15 kitchen-equipped cottages, lawn games, a convenience store, and a launderette.

GETTING THERE

The reserve is 70 kilometers (one hour) south of Argentia via Route 100. It's 170 kilometers (two hours) southwest of St. John's via Route 1 and Route 92.

Central and Western Newfoundland

Visualize the island of Newfoundland as not one island but two, similarly shaped but different in size—a mammoth main island and a smaller one. This chapter covers the former—everything west of the Avalon Peninsula. The "two

islands" are linked by an isthmus that begins an hour's drive west from St. John's. Beyond the turnoff to the delightfully named village of Come by Chance, the TransCanada Highway enters the meaty part of the island. Think of this highway as a long Main Street. The horseshoe-shaped route edges the interior and connects the Avalon Peninsula with Channel-Port-aux-Basques—a 905-kilometer journey. Well-marked side roads split off the main highway and whisk drivers onto the peninsulas. Aside from the Burin Peninsula's efficient Route 210 and the Northern Peninsula's relatively uncomplicated Route 430, the other side roads to the peninsulas and coastlines meander interminably.

The appeal of raw wilderness aside, this vast part of Newfoundland caters to numerous interests. Majestic icebergs wander into fjords and coves on the northern coastlines. All along the seacoasts, photogenic lighthouses perch atop precipitous cliffs overlooking the surf. Sightseers line up for boat tours led by knowledgeable skippers or academically trained guides, whose vessels nose among whales, seals, and icebergs. If you're interested in a quick trip to France, you can visit a remnant of the long-ago age of exploration: Fortune on the Burin Peninsula is just a two-hour boat ride from St-Pierre, the capital of France's archipelago province of St-Pierre and Miquelon. The ancient world heaved and formed richly diverse landscapes at Gros Morne National Park. A millennium ago, the Vikings arrived and established a coastal camp (North America's first European settlement), now re-created at L'Anse aux Meadows National Historic Site.

PLANNING YOUR TIME

While the previous chapter covered a small corner of the province, in this chapter, distances will prove to be important when planning how and where to spend your time. For

Highlights

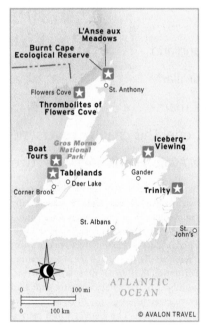

★ **Trinity:** Step back in time at this quintessential Newfoundland village with brightly painted, saltbox-style houses lining its narrow lanes (page 43).

★ **Iceberg-Viewing:** You can see icebergs from various points along the northern Newfoundland coast, but one of the most reliable spots is Twillingate (page 50).

★ **Tablelands:** This geological phenomenon is too complicated to describe in a single sentence—but you'll be lost for words scrambling through its moonlike terrain anyway (page 63).

★ **Boat Tours in Gros Morne National Park:** Take to Western Brook Pond in Gros Morne National Park for neck-straining views of an ancient, glacially carved fjord (page 65).

★ **Thrombolites of Flowers Cove:** Never heard of thrombolites? Most people haven't. But don't blink—even though they occur in only two places on Earth, they're not signposted as you drive north along the Viking Trail (page 71).

★ **L'Anse aux Meadows:** Follow in the footsteps of the Vikings by exploring the tip of the Northern Peninsula (page 73).

★ **Burnt Cape Ecological Reserve:** Scenic in a wild and rugged Newfoundland kind of way, this remote limestone outcrop is home to more rare and endangered species of plants than anywhere else in Atlantic Canada (page 76).

Central and Western Newfoundland

example, from St. John's, it's 640 kilometers to Deer Lake, 905 kilometers to the ferry terminal at Port-aux-Basques, and almost 1,100 kilometers to St. Anthony at the tip of the Northern Peninsula.

The time you spend in the central and western regions of Newfoundland obviously ties in with your travels to St. John's and the Avalon Peninsula. Traveling to the Bonavista Peninsula and villages like Trinity can be a two-day trip from the capital, but travel any farther west and you're committed to driving clear across the island. If you're catching the ferry from Port-aux-Basques, allow at least five days to get there from the capital. This

would allow a night at Trinity, a detour from the TransCanada Highway to go iceberg-viewing at Twillingate, and a couple of days exploring Gros Morne National Park, where highlights include hiking through the Tablelands and taking a boat tour on Western Brook Pond.

What this five-day suggestion doesn't take into consideration is the Northern Peninsula, which is one of my favorite places in all of Canada. It's 470 amazing kilometers stretch from Deer Lake to the tip of the peninsula. With time spent exploring the region's beautiful coastline, as well as stops at the thrombolites of Flowers Cove, L'Anse aux Meadows, and Burnt Cape Ecological Reserve, add at least four days to your cross-province schedule from St. John's to Port-aux-Basques. If you're returning a rental vehicle to St. John's, give the stretch of highway south of Deer Lake a miss, but still add two days to the total trip. By flying in and out of Deer Lake, you can concentrate your time in Gros Morne National Park and the Northern Peninsula—an ideal scenario for outdoors lovers.

Burin Peninsula and Vicinity

The 200-kilometer-long Burin Peninsula angles like a kicking boot off Newfoundland's southeastern coastline. The peninsula's interior is a primeval, barren moonscape—if the moon had water, that is, for every hollow and depression in these barrens is filled with bogs, marshes, and ponds. But the coastline rims the edge of the Grand Banks, historically one of the most fertile fishing regions in North America. Along the shore are scattered fishing villages and several burgeoning towns. Marystown, one of the fastest-growing towns in the province, is supported by one of the largest fish-processing plants in eastern Canada, and its shipyard supplies vessels to the booming North Atlantic oil industry. St. Lawrence is the exception to the region; as Canada's only producer of the mineral fluorite, it has relied on mining as much as on marine-related industries. For the most part, however, fishing has been the mainstay of the peninsula's communities since the 1500s.

BOAT HARBOUR

A cottage industry here produces hand-hooked scenic mats made of reused fabric scraps. The mats and other homemade wares are sold at reasonable prices at the Placentia West Craft Shop (Rte. 210, 709/443-2312; summer daily 8:30am-6pm), about one kilometer south of the Boat Harbour intersection.

Getting There

Boat Harbour is 270 kilometers (3.5 hours) west of St. John's via the TransCanada Highway and Route 210.

BURIN

Near the "heel" of the boot-shaped peninsula, Burin, settled in the early 1700s, lies in the lee of offshore islands. The islands generally protect the town from the open Atlantic, though they weren't enough to stop a destructive tidal wave in 1929. The islands also were a refuge for pirates, who could escape their pursuers among the dangerous channels. During his mapping expeditions of the Newfoundland coast in the 1760s, Captain James Cook used Burin as a seasonal headquarters. A high hill above the town, where watch was kept for smugglers and illegal fishing, still bears his name—Cook's Lookout.

In early July, the Festival of Folk Song and Dance (709/891-2655) kicks off three days of Irish-inspired music making, children's games, seafood meals, and craft shows and sales. The festival ranks among Newfoundland's most popular heritage events.

A friendly accommodation is the Wheelhouse Inn (204 Main St., 709/891-2000 or 877/891-3810, www.wheelhouseinn. com; $89-109 s or d). The three guest rooms are spacious and modern, each with a private bathroom that holds a shower/tub combo, Wi-Fi Internet access, and a TV/DVD combo. Other amenities include a lounge with a fireplace and a recreation room anchored with a pool table. Rates include a cooked breakfast.

Getting There

Burin is about 60 kilometers (one hour) south of Boat Harbour via Route 210. It's about 310 kilometers (4-4.5 hours) southwest of St. John's via Route 1 and Route 210.

GRAND BANK

Grand Bank, on the "toe" of the Burin boot, is the best known of the peninsula's towns. Settled in the 1650s by the French and taken over by the British in the early 1700s, Grand Bank (pop. 2,500) has always been associated with the rich fishing grounds of the same name, the Grand Banks to the south and west of Newfoundland.

The Heritage Walk visits the province's largest number of Queen Anne-style homes outside of St. John's. The historic district's architectural treasures include the 1905 Masonic Lodge, the 1917 Thorndyke House (with its Masonic symbolism integrated into the interior design), and the George C. Harris House (16 Water St., 709/832-1574; July-Aug. daily 10am-4pm; adult $3). The latter is a 1908 Queen Anne building housing the town's museum. Complementing the Heritage Walk are the Nature Trail, leading to a lookout and salmon spawning beds, and the Marine Trail, which closely follows the shoreline of Fortune Bay to the Mariners' Memorial.

After extensive renovations in 2011, the Provincial Seamen's Museum (54 Marine Dr., 709/832-1484; May-early Oct. Mon.-Sat. 9am-4:30pm, Sun. noon-4:45pm; adult $2.50) is difficult to miss. Styled as an angular white sailing ship, the museum has exhibits on the Grand Banks fisheries and maritime history, with photographs, ship models, and other artifacts.

Getting There

Grand Bank is almost 60 kilometers (one hour) west of Burin via Routes 210 and 222. Grand Bank is 360 kilometers (4.5 hours) southwest of St. John's, via Route 1 and Route 210.

ST-PIERRE AND MIQUELON

Centuries of fierce British and French battles ended in the mid-1700s with Britain's dominance firmly stamped across eastern Canada—*except* on St-Pierre and Miquelon, a trio of islands 25 kilometers south of the Newfoundland mainland. Today, this geopolitical oddity is not part of Atlantic Canada, but rather a *département* of France and the last toehold of France's once-vast holdings in North America.

St-Pierre and Miquelon are French in all regards. Unlike traveling to French regions of Canada, there is a lot more than a foreign language to deal with. Canadians must show photo identification, such as a driver's license or passport. Entry for all other nationalities mirrors entry requirements for France; in other words, a passport is required for U.S. citizens.

Legal tender is the euro (€), but some (not all) businesses accept U.S. and Canadian dollars at fair bank rates. Electrical current throughout St-Pierre and Miquelon is 220 volts, although the bigger hotels have converters.

The islands even have their own time zone—30 minutes ahead of Newfoundland time.

Sights

St-Pierre and Miquelon consists of three islands, with a combined land area of about 242 square kilometers. Tiny St-Pierre is the name of the smallest island, as well as a bustling town (pop. 6,300). The topography of this triangular island includes hills, bogs, and ponds in the north, and lowlands in the south. The larger islands are Miquelon, which is home to a village of the same name (pop. 600), and uninhabited Petite Miquelon (also called Langdale). These two islands are joined by a sand-dune isthmus.

The capital, St-Pierre, is the most popular destination. It dates to the early 1600s, when French fishermen, mainly from Brittany, worked offshore. The port's mood and appearance are pervasively French, with bistros, cafés, bars, brasseries, wrought-iron balconies, and an abundance of Gallic pride. St-Pierre borders a sheltered harbor filled with colorful fishing boats and backed by narrow lanes that radiate uphill from the harbor. The cemetery, two blocks inland from rue du 11 Novembre, has an interesting arrangement of above-ground graves, similar to those in New Orleans.

One of the islands' greatest attractions, of course, is the low duty rates on French wines and other goods. Visitors may bring back $200 worth of duty-free purchases after a 48-hour visit. You'll find shops with French wines, perfumes, and jewelry.

Accommodations

Because the number of guest rooms is limited, make all lodging arrangements before arriving.

Auberge Saint-Pierre (16 rue Georges Daguerre, 508/41-40-86, www.aubergesaint-pierre.fr; €78 s, €88-105 d) has clean and comfortable guest rooms with wireless Internet access throughout. Rates include a hot and cold breakfast of French specialties.

Among the dozen small hotels, pensions, and B&Bs, the largest lodging is the 43-room l'Hôtel Robert (14 rue du 11 Novembre, 508/41-24-19, www.hotelrobert.com; €118-128 s or d), along the harbor front and within walking distance of the ferry wharf. Having hosted the American gangster Al Capone in the 1920s, this red-brick lodging itself oozes historic charm, yet the renovated rooms have contemporary furnishings.

Food

Make your way through the streets of St-Pierre and it's difficult not to be tempted by the sweet smells coming from the many patisseries and cafés. A favorite is Les Delices de Josephine (10, Rue du General Leclerc, 508/41-20-27; Mon.-Sat. noon-6pm, Sun. 3:30pm-6pm; lunches €5-11), which has delicious coffee, a great selection of teas, pastries made daily from scratch, and a selection of hot lunch items such as quiche.

One of the best choices for a casual meal is Le Feu de Braise (14 rue Albert Briand, 508/41-91-60; daily noon-2:30pm and 6pm-10pm; €13-20), a bright room offering a menu dominated by classic French bistro-style dishes.

Information

Once on the island, the best source of information is the St-Pierre & Miquelon Tourist Office (rue Antoine Soucy, 508/41-02-00, www.tourisme-saint-pierre-et-miquelon.com). The website has links to island accommodations as well as tour bundles that include accommodations.

Getting There

Air Saint Pierre (902/873-3566, www.air-saintpierre.com) flies year-round between St-Pierre and St. John's for $414 round-trip. The airline also flies into St-Pierre from Halifax, Sydney (Nova Scotia), and Montréal.

Le Cabestan (709/832-3455 or 855/832-3455; www.saintpierreferry.ca, round-trip adult C$93, senior $88, child C$58) is a high-speed passenger ferry that operates between Fortune, on the Burin Peninsula, and St-Pierre once daily in July and August and four days a week April-June and in September.

The Bonavista Peninsula rises off the eastern coastline as a broad, bent finger covered with verdant woods, farmlands, and rolling hills. Paved Route 230 runs along the peninsula's length, from the TransCanada Highway to the town of Bonavista at the tip; Route 235 returns to Highway 1 along the peninsula's west side.

CLARENVILLE

Founded in 1890, Clarenville, along the TransCanada Highway, 190 kilometers from St. John's, serves as the gateway to the Bonavista Peninsula. The town is relatively new compared to the rest of Newfoundland and offers few reasons to stop other than to rest your head for the night.

Along the TransCanada Highway are two larger motels. From St. John's, the first of these is the Clarenville Inn (134 TransCanada Hwy., 709/466-7911 or 877/466-7911, www.clarenvilleinn.ca; $105 s, $115 d), which fronts the highway, offering 63 rooms with wireless Internet and an outdoor heated pool. One of the best things about this lodging is Bacalao, a restaurant with surprisingly creative

Newfoundland cooking (daily for breakfast, lunch, and dinner; $15-26). In town itself, the Restland Motel (Memorial Dr., 709/466-7636, www.restlandmotel.ca; from $95 s or d) has a mix of midsized air-conditioned motel rooms and kitchen-equipped units. On site a pub, and across the road is a shopping mall.

Getting There

Clarenville is 190 kilometers (two hours) northwest of St. John's via Route 1.

★ TRINITY

Just three years after John Cabot bumped into Newfoundland, Portugal commissioned mariners Gaspar and Miguel Côrte-Real to search for a passage to China. That mission failed, but Gaspar accidentally sailed into Trinity Bay on Trinity Sunday in 1501. In 1558, merchants from England's West Country founded a settlement on the same site, making it even older than St. Augustine, Florida.

The attractive village of Trinity (pop. 400) has changed little since the late 1800s. White picket fences, small gardens, and historic

Many of Trinity's historic buildings are open to the public.

homes are everywhere. The best photo vantage point of Trinity is from the Route 239 coastal spur, the narrow road also known as Courthouse Road. The road peels across the headlands, turns a quick corner, and suddenly overlooks the seaport. Ease into the turn so you can savor the view. (To get a photograph, park your car in the village and walk back up the road.) Once down in the village proper, park your car and explore on foot.

Sights

The **Trinity Visitor Centre** (Rte. 239, 709/729-0592; mid-May-mid-Oct. daily 9:30am-5pm), in a handsomely restored building, has historical exhibits about the village. **Mercantile Premises** (West St., 709/464-2042; mid-May-mid-Oct. daily 9:30am-5pm) is a restored 1820s general store. In the 1800s, Emma Hiscock and her two daughters lived in the restored mustard-and-green **Hiscock House** (Church Rd., mid-May-mid-Oct. daily 9:30am-5pm), a block inland from the government wharf. They operated a forge, retail store, and telegraph office in the saltbox-style house. These three attractions are operated by the province; combined admission is adult $6, child $3.

The following buildings, scattered through the village, are looked after by the Trinity Historical Society (709/464-3599). They are each open mid-May to mid-October (daily 9:30am-5pm, $20 for all four buildings, children free). **Lester Garland House** is an imposing Georgian-style red-brick mansion that has been restored to its 1820s appearance and now houses a museum. The **Green Family Forge** (Church Rd.), in a restored 1895 building, is a blacksmith museum displaying more than 1,500 tools, products, and other artifacts of the blacksmith trade. Also on Church Road is an 1880 saltbox-style house that now serves as the **Trinity Society Museum,** displaying more than 2,000 fishing, mercantile, medical, and fire-fighting artifacts. Although there has been a cooperage (barrel maker) in Trinity since the 1700s, **The Cooperage** is a modern replica of what a similar business would have looked like in times gone by. In summer, you can watch coopers here creating barrels and other wooden objects using traditional techniques.

Entertainment and Events

The summer solstice kicks off Rising Tide Theatre's **Summer in the Bight** (709/464-3232, www.risingtidetheatre.com), presenting original musical and dramatic

a performance by Summer in the Bight

productions written and performed by some of Newfoundland's best writers and actors. The theater is a re-created fishing shed on Green's Point, at the eastern side of the village. Performances are scheduled 2-3 times a week and cost $26 ($39 for the dinner theater).

Accommodations

Right on the water, the ★ **Artisan Inn** (57 High St., 709/464-3377 or 877/464-7700, www. trinityvacations.com; May-mid-Oct.; $129-195 s or d) is set up as a retreat for artists—if views from the oceanfront studio don't inspire you, nothing will—but everyone is welcome. It offers two en suite rooms and a kitchen-equipped suite. The adjacent Campbell House holds an additional three guest rooms. Rates include breakfast, and dinner is available at the in-house **Twine Loft** with advance notice.

Getting There

Trinity is 70 kilometers (one hour) northeast of Clarenville along Route 230. From St. John's, Trinity is 270 kilometers (3.5 hours) west on Route 1 and north on Route 230.

PORT UNION

The only town in Canada to have been established by a labor union, Port Union lies 32 kilometers past Trinity. The oldest part of town is across the bay from the fish-processing plant. Turn right as you enter the village and you'll soon find yourself in Port Union South, passing through a narrow street of boarded-up company warehouses. Beyond these is **Port Union Historical Museum** (Main St., 709/469-2728; mid-June-Aug. daily 11am-5pm; adult $2, child $1), housed in a waterfront 1917 railway station. Once you've read up on the town's history, backtrack and take a left turn through a narrow rock cleft to Bungalow Hill for sweeping harbor views.

Getting There

From Trinity, it's 30 kilometers (30 minutes) northeast on Route 230 to Port Union. To get to Port Union from St. John's, take Highway 1 west and Route 230 north for a total of 290 kilometers (four hours).

BONAVISTA

Fifty kilometers up Route 230 from Trinity, Bonavista (pop. 5,000) is a surprisingly large town that sprawls across the far reaches of the Bonavista Peninsula. The town began in the 1600s as a French fishing port, but many believe **Cape Bonavista,** six kilometers north of town, was the first landfall of Giovanni

looking down to the Artisan Inn

Caboto (better known as John Cabot), who visited the region in 1497.

Sights

Downtown Bonavista centers on a harbor filled with fishing boats and surrounded by a colorful array of homes and businesses. The historic highlight is Ryan Premises (corner of Ryan's Hill and Old Catalina Rd., 709/468-1600; June-Aug. daily 10am-6pm; adult $4, senior $3.50, child $2), where merchant James Ryan established his salt-fish enterprise in the mid-1800s. The site's collection of white clapboard buildings includes a fish store and a re-created retail shop. Across the road is the original manager's residence. All buildings are filled with exhibits and artifacts of the era. In the salt shed, local crafters demonstrate such skills as furniture making; their goods can be purchased in the retail shop.

Also worth searching out downtown is The Elephant Shop (8 Ackerman's Ln., 709/468-8145; May-Oct. Tues.-Sun. 11am-5pm), a wooden residence dating to the late 1800s that has been transformed into a boutique selling high-quality clothing and jewelry, and well worth visiting for both the history and shopping experience. The spacious attic of the home has been transformed into The Aleksandrs International Gallery of Fine Art (same contact information and hours), with a high ceiling, funky wall angles, and contemporary do-over creating a unique space where original art from varied destinations such as the High Arctic and Australia is displayed.

Signposted through town, the 1871 Mockbeggar Plantation (Mockbeggar Rd., 709/468-7300; mid-May-mid-Oct. daily 9:30am-5pm; adult $6, senior $4, child $3) is a whitewashed waterfront building surrounded by a white picket fence. It has been a residence, carpenter's shop, and fish store.

Beyond Mockbeggar Plantation, the photogenic 1843 Cape Bonavista Lighthouse (Rte. 230, 709/468-7444; mid-May-mid-Oct. daily 9:30am-5pm; adult $6, senior $4, child $3) crowns a steep and rocky headland. The keeper's quarters inside the red-and-white-striped tower have been restored to the 1870 period. A climb up steep steps leads to the original catoptric light with Argand oil burners and reflectors.

Accommodations

Bonavista makes a pleasant day trip from Trinity, but if you want to stay longer, there are numerous options. The most luxurious by far, and one of the finest accommodations in all of Newfoundland, is ★ Elizabeth J. Cottages (Harris St., 709/468-5035 or 866/468-5035, www.elizabethjcottages.com; May-Oct.; $325 s or d). The cottages enjoy an absolute oceanfront setting on the edge of town; their design was inspired by the old saltbox homes still common throughout the region, but beyond the layout, no expense has been spared in creating a luxurious environment in which to soak up the sweeping ocean views. The two-bedroom units are awash in natural light and feature niceties such as freshly baked bread upon arrival, 650-thread-count sheets, and plush bathrobes. Other features include private decks with slick outdoor furniture and barbecues, modem hookups, TV/DVD combos, and laundry facilities.

If your tastes are a little simpler, the four Oceanside Cabins (Cape Shore Rd., 709/468-7771; $100-120 s or d), with basic kitchens and Wi-Fi, should suffice.

Getting There

Allow 20 minutes to reach Bonavista from Port Union, which is 20 kilometers south via Route 230. To get to Bonavista from St. John's, take Highway 1 west and Route 230 north for a total of 310 kilometers (just over four hours).

Clarenville to Deer Lake

It's 450 kilometers from Clarenville to Deer Lake. The TransCanada Highway linking these two towns cuts across the interior in a rambling inland path, sometimes angling north to touch a deeply carved bay or reaching into the interior to amble amid the plateau's seemingly endless stretches of tree-blanketed hills. The best chance to get up close and personal with this region is Terra Nova National Park, but there are also many worthwhile detours, such as to Twillingate, famous for its iceberg-watching tours.

TERRA NOVA NATIONAL PARK

The TransCanada Highway enters Terra Nova National Park 35 kilometers north of Clarenville, and for the next 50 kilometers it travels within the park boundary. But to really see the park, divert from the highway to remote bodies of fish-filled freshwater, through forests inhabited by moose and bears, and to the rugged coastline where kayakers glide through protected water and bald eagles soar overhead.

Park Entry

You don't need a pass to drive through the national park, but if you plan on stopping for any reason, you must pay admission (adult $6, senior $5, child $3). Your payment is valid until 4pm the following day.

Park Visitor Centre

Make your first stop the Park Visitor Centre (709/533-2942; mid-May-June Thurs.-Mon. 10am-4pm, July-Aug. daily 10am-6pm, Sept.-mid-Oct. daily Thurs.-Mon. 10am-4pm; free with park admission). Overlooking Newman Sound at Salton's Brook, it is one kilometer off the TransCanada Highway, 35 kilometers north of where it first enters the park. The center features small aquariums, touch tanks, a live feed from an underwater camera,

exhibits on the various marine habitats within the park, interactive computer displays, and films, plus a restaurant and gift shop. The center's gift shop sells topographical maps of the park and stocks books about the province's flora, fauna, and attractions.

Hiking

More than a dozen trails thread through the park, providing some 60 kilometers of hiking. Most are uncomplicated loop routes that meander easily for an hour's walk beneath tree canopies. From the Park Visitor Centre, the one-kilometer Heritage Trail leads along Salton's Brook, and a three-kilometer (one-way) trail leads to picturesque and quiet Blue Hill Pond. Another three-kilometer trail follows the edge of Sandy Pond, starting from 13 kilometers south of the Park Visitor Centre. The longest trek, the 55-kilometer Outport Trail, requires backcountry camping skills. Most hikers spend one or two nights on the trail, which is notable for the opportunities it affords to see icebergs and whales.

Water Sports

At the Park Visitor Centre, you'll find a wharf, from where tour boats and kayakers depart for trips along Newman Sound. Handy amenities at the wharf include washrooms with hot showers and coin laundry facilities. Take a guided trip with Coastal Connections (709/533-2196, www.coastalconnections.ca). The 2.5-hour Eco Discovery Cruise (adult $65, senior $55, child $35) noses among the fjord fingers looking for seabirds and marine life while teaching passengers about the park and its natural history.

Take a break from the saltwater by planning to spend time at Sandy Pond, a shallow body of water 13 kilometers south of the Park Visitor Centre and 12 kilometers north of the southern park boundary. This day-use area has canoe and kayak rentals (709/677-2221;

$10 for 30 minutes), allows swimming, and is encircled by a three-kilometer walking trail (allow one hour).

Accommodations and Food

While there are no accommodations within park boundaries, the following two options lie on the edge of the park.

The village of Charlottetown occupies a pocket of oceanfront land 15 kilometers north of the park, outside the official park boundary. Here you find the trim **Clode Sound Motel** (709/664-3146, www.clodesound.com; May-Oct.; $110-130 s or d). It has 18 rooms and a three-bedroom cottage ($200), an outdoor swimming pool, a playground, a tennis court, and barbecue pits. Also on the premises is a highly regarded restaurant that serves wonderful desserts created with apples from the motel's 90-year-old orchard.

Just beyond the south end of the park is **Terra Nova Resort** (TransCanada Hwy., 709/543-2525, www.terranovagolf.com; May-Oct.; from $155 s or d), a full-service resort built alongside the Twin Rivers Golf Course, where golfers get to walk some of Canada's finest fairways for the bargain price of $60 midweek and $69 on weekends. Other amenities include tennis courts, an outdoor heated pool, hiking trails, the **Clode Sound Dining Room** (May-Oct. daily for breakfast, lunch, and dinner; $26-36), and a pub. The 83 guest rooms feature solid furnishings and a contemporary feel. Children are catered to with a schedule of activities that includes treasure hunts, craft sessions, and picnic lunches.

Camping

Wooded **Newman Sound Campground** (tents $28, hookups $32) has 387 full- and semi-serviced campsites, kitchen shelters, heated washrooms with hot showers, a Nature House (June-Sept. daily 10am-5pm), a launderette, and a daily interpretive program. Reservations are taken for 40 percent of the sites through Parks Canada (877/737-3783, www.pccamping.ca). The cost is $11 per

reservation, plus the camping fee. The campground turnoff is 30 kilometers north of the southern park boundary. A 4.5-kilometer trail along Newman Sound links the campground with the Park Visitor Centre.

From the park's northern edge, head five kilometers east on Route 310 to reach **Malady Head Campground** ($22.50 per site). The facility has a kitchen/activity area and playground.

Getting There

The entrance to Terra Nova National Park is 65 kilometers (40 minutes) north of Clarenville via Highway 1. To get to the park from St. John's, take Highway 1 west and north for 250 kilometers (three hours).

GANDER

The town of Gander is halfway between Newfoundland's two largest cities (350 kilometers from St. John's and 357 kilometers from Corner Brook). It was founded in 1951, when the military decided to convert Gander Airport to civilian operations, and

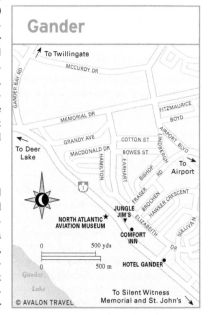

so it's fitting that the main attractions today revolve around air travel.

Gateway to North America

When aircraft cross the Atlantic Ocean from Europe, they enter North American airspace somewhere off the coast of Newfoundland. In the early days of aviation, this meant that the planes needed somewhere to refuel, and so Gander grew as a stopping point for all types of aviation. Although commercial transatlantic flights no longer need to refuel at Gander, the airport retains its importance, such as after the terrorist attacks of September 11, 2001, when 39 commercial planes carrying more than 6,500 crew and passengers were diverted to Gander. Even if you're not departing on one of the scheduled Air Canada or Provincial Airlines flights, it's worth dropping by Gander International Airport, on the northeastern side of downtown, to view the many displays and memorabilia through the main terminal.

Gleaming full-size models of World War II Hudson, Voodoo, and Canso water bombers, a Beech 18 aircraft, and a reconstructed De Havilland Tiger Moth greet visitors to the North Atlantic Aviation Museum (135 TransCanada Hwy., 709/256-2923; mid-May-June Mon.-Fri. 9am-5pm, July-Aug. daily 9am-9pm, Sept. Mon.-Fri. 9am-5pm; adult $6, senior and child $5). Inside, exhibits on Gander's strategic role in World War II and the development of transatlantic aviation include early equipment, uniforms, photographs, and a reconstructed DC-3 cockpit.

The Silent Witness Memorial, four kilometers east of town and one kilometer south along an unpaved road, marks the site of an aviation disaster. On a cold December day in 1985, the airport was a scheduled refueling stop for a DC-8 flight from the Middle East. The flight carried the U.S. 101st Airborne Division, better known as the Screaming Eagles, who were returning home from a United Nations peacekeeping mission in the Sinai. The plane, with 248 soldiers and an eight-member crew, crashed shortly after takeoff between the highway and Gander Lake. A group of statues, of an American soldier and two children, backed by Canadian, U.S., and Newfoundland flags, overlooks the lake. The memorial spreads across the rocky hillside, and flower bouquets lie here and there.

Accommodations and Food

Gander is a convenient stop for travelers crossing Newfoundland's interior, and it provides a wide choice of accommodations. The two-story Comfort Inn (112 TransCanada Hwy., 709/256-3535, www.comfortinn.com; $105 s, $115 d, including a continental breakfast buffet) has 64 spacious and relatively modern guest rooms. Facilities include wireless Internet and a small fitness room. Hotel Gander (TransCanada Hwy., 709/256-3931 or 800/563-2988, www.hotelgander.com; $108-166 s or d) is older, but it has 152 rooms and suites, a restaurant (daily 7am-2pm and 5pm-9pm; $13-27), a lounge with entertainment, an indoor pool, and an exercise room.

Beside the Comfort Inn is Jungle Jim's (112 TransCanada Hwy., 709/651-3444; daily 11am-11pm; $13-22). If you can get the waitstaff's attention through the vines and bamboo decorations, order dishes such as fish-and-chips or ribs.

Getting There

It's almost 150 kilometers (1.5 hours) northwest to Gander from Clarenville via Route 1. From St. John's, it's a 330-kilometer (four-hour) drive on Route 1.

NORTH TO TWILLINGATE

From Gander, Route 330 heads north to Gander Bay, where Route 331 curves farther northwest and lopes onto the northern archipelago as Route 340, better known as the Road to the Shore.

Boyd's Cove

Boyd's Cove, 70 kilometers north of Gander, at the intersection of Routes 331 and 340, is a small village with a large attraction: Beothuk

Interpretation Site (709/656-3114; mid-May-early Oct. daily 10am-5:30pm; adult $4). Designed to mimic the shapes of 300-year-old Beothuk dwellings, the center lies at the end of a two-kilometer gravel road. The detour is worth it, though, for the artifacts, dioramas, films, and exquisitely expressive paintings depicting the history of the Beothuk people. Take the 20-minute walk down to the site of the 17th-century Beothuk encampment, excavated in the early 1980s. Eleven house pits, clearly defined by earthen walls, were discovered here, along with countless artifacts, such as beads, stone tools, and iron.

GETTING THERE

From Gander, it's 70 kilometers (one hour) north to Boyd's Cove via Route 330 and Route 331. To get to Boyd's Cove from St. John's, it's a 400-kilometer (five-hour) drive on Route 1, Route 330, and Route 331.

TWILLINGATE

Beyond Boyd's Cove, causeways link an archipelago of islands lying close to the mainland. Along the way, narrow Route 430 passes farmland (where you might catch a glimpse of the rare Newfoundland pony); gentle, island-filled bays; and tiny outports to finish at South and North Twillingate islands. The archipelago's most northwesterly point, the islands are washed by the Atlantic and shouldered by Notre Dame Bay. The road crosses the southern island and eases into the tiny port at Twillingate Harbour.

Cross the causeway to Twillingate (pop. 3,500) on the northwestern island. Main Street runs alongside the scenic harbor before it zips north and climbs to Long Point.

Sights and Recreation
TWILLINGATE MUSEUM

If you're interested in local lore, stop at Twillingate Museum (1 St. Peter's Church Rd., 709/884-2825; mid-May-early Oct. daily 9am-9pm; adult $4, child $2). The whitewashed wooden building sits back from the road and is bordered by a white picket fence—altogether as proper as a former Anglican manse should be. The museum's extensive exhibits include historic fishing gear and tools, antique dolls, and several rare Dorset Inuit artifacts. One room is devoted to the career of Dr. John Olds, Twillingate's famous expatriate surgeon who came from the United States to pioneer medicine in remote Newfoundland. The intriguing medical artifacts include a collection of early 20th-century pharmaceuticals and glass eyes.

★ ICEBERG-VIEWING

Icebergs, which wander offshore and sometimes ditch at land's end in Notre Dame Bay, are one of Twillingate's main claims to fame. If you're interested in getting up close, take one of the three daily cruises offered by Twillingate Island Boat Tours, based at the Iceberg Shop (50 Main St., 709/884-2242 or 800/611-2374, www.icebergtours.ca), on the south side of the harbor (turn right as you enter town). Tours operate May through September with departures daily at 9:30am, 1pm, and 4pm. They are operated by Cecil Stockley, who steers the MV *Iceberg Alley* to wherever icebergs have grounded in the vicinity of Twillingate. The tours are adult $55, child $35, and last two hours.

You may also see an offshore iceberg from Back Harbour, a short walk starting from the museum and passing by a cemetery. Otherwise, head for Long Point, the high rocky promontory that juts into the Atlantic Ocean beside Notre Dame Bay. To get there, take Main Street around the harbor (past the museum and Harbour Lights Inn) and follow the road all the way to Long Point for the best land-based iceberg viewing in the area. In addition to a photogenic lighthouse, trails lead down through the boulder-strewn point and across to a couple of pebbly beaches.

Accommodations

Visitors to Twillingate often find themselves captivated by the town's charm, and because of this, numerous accommodations can be found. ★ Harbour Lights Inn (189 Main

icebergs off the coast of Twillingate

St., 709/884-2763, www.harbourlightsinn. ca; Apr.-late Oct.; $105-135 s or d) is a restored early-19th-century home overlooking the harbor. The inn features nine guest rooms decorated in smart colors and appealing furnishings, each with an en suite bathroom and wireless Internet access; two rooms have whirlpool baths. Rates include a cooked breakfast.

If you prefer more privacy, consider Cabins by the Sea (11 Hugh Ln., 709/884-2158, www.cabinsbythesea.com; $89 s or d), comprising seven small self-contained cabins overlooking the ocean. If the timing is right, you may see icebergs.

Getting There

To get to Twillingate from Boyd's Cove, take Route 340 north for 40 kilometers (40 minutes). From St. John's, it's a 445-kilometer (six-hour) drive west on Route 1, then north on Route 330, Route 331, and Route 340.

GRAND FALLS-WINDSOR

For the sake of government, the two towns of Grand Falls-Windsor have been merged to form one municipality, but keep in mind that Windsor lies north of the TransCanada Highway and Grand Falls south. Grand Falls-Windsor lies almost exactly halfway along the Newfoundland leg of the TransCanada Highway: St. John's is 428 kilometers to the east, and Port-aux-Basques is 476 kilometers to the west.

Sights

Grand Falls offers the most sightseeing. Turn south off the highway at Cromer Avenue to the Mary March Provincial Museum (24 St. Catherine St., 709/292-4522; early May-Sept. Mon.-Sat. 9am-4:30pm, Sun. noon-4:30pm; adult $2.50), where exhibits about the area's Beothuk people, natural history, geology, and regional industry fill the modern center.

The town is aptly named for its Grand Falls, a white-water gush of rapids across the Exploits River as it speeds alongside the town. To see the falls, take Scott Avenue off the TransCanada Highway to the south, and you'll find yourself in the heart of downtown Grand Falls. Cross the river at a narrow wooden bridge at the now-closed pulp and paper mill and look north for the best views. You can get a close look at the salmon

Icebergs on Parade

The spectacular icebergs that float past Newfoundland and Labrador every summer originate from southwestern Greenland's ice cap, where great chunks of ice calve off the coast and cascade into the bone-chilling Davis Strait. The young bergs eventually drift out to the Labrador Sea, where powerful currents route them south along the watery route known as Iceberg Alley. The parade usually starts in March, peaks in June and July, and in rare cases continues into November.

Although no one actually counts icebergs, an educated guess has 10,000-30,000 of them migrating down from the north annually. Of those, about 1,400-2,000 make it all the way to the Gulf Stream's warm waters, where they finally melt away after a two- to four-year, 3,200-kilometer journey.

No two bergs are exactly the same. Some appear distinctly white. Others may be turquoise, green, or blue. Sizes vary too: A "growler" is the smallest, about the size of a dory, and weighs about 1,000 tons. A "bergy bit" weighs more, about 10,000 tons. A typical "small" iceberg looms 5-15 meters above water level and weighs about 100,000 tons. A "large" ice mass will be 51-75 meters high and weigh 100-300 million tons. Generally, you'll see the largest bergs—looking like magnificent castles embellished with towers and turrets—farther north; the ice mountains diminish in size as they float south and eventually melt. No matter what the size, what you see is just a fraction of the whole—some 90 percent of the iceberg's mass is hidden beneath the water.

Occasionally, a wandering berg may be trapped at land's edge or wedged within coves and slender bays. Should you be tempted to go in for a closer look, approach with caution. As it melts and its equilibrium readjusts, an iceberg may roll over. And melting bergs also often fracture, throwing ice chips and knife-sharp splinters in all directions.

The best website for information and tracking data is www.icebergfinder.com, which includes up-to-date satellite images of where icebergs are located.

that inhabit the river by continuing beyond the bridge to the **Salmonid Interpretation Centre** (709/489-7350; mid-June-mid-Sept. daily 8am to dusk; adult $4, child $2.50). The main floor's exhibits explain the salmon's life cycle and habitat, while on the observation level you can watch the migratory salmon through the viewing windows.

Accommodations

On the residential outskirts of Windsor, **Carriage House Inn** (181 Grenfell Heights, 709/489-7185 or 800/563-7133, www.carriage-houseinn.ca; $89-129 s or d) comprises 10 spick-and-span guest rooms, with full breakfast included in the rates. Outside you'll find a covered veranda, a pool, a sundeck, and stables.

Mount Peyton Hotel (214 Lincoln Rd., 709/489-2251 or 800/563-4894, www.mount-peyton.com; $105-150 s or d) has an array of accommodations on both sides of the TransCanada Highway, including 102 hotel

rooms, 32 motel rooms, and 16 housekeeping units. The motel's dining room is known locally for its seafood, locally grown vegetables, and dessert, made up of berries in all forms.

★ **Hotel Robin Hood** (78 Lincoln Rd., 709/489-5324, www.hotelrobinhood.com; $115-135 s or d) is Grand Falls-Windsor's most appealing motel. Small and charming, it's set off from the road and run by a couple from Nottingham, England. The 14 rooms, all air-conditioned and with private baths and larger flat-screen TVs, are comfortable and spacious. Rates include continental breakfast.

Food

On the south side of the highway, the main street of Grand Falls offers a couple of reasonable dining options. Opposite the distinctively arched town hall entrance is **Daily Grind** (12 High St., 709/489-5252; Mon.-Fri. 7am-8pm, Sat. 10am-6pm, Sun. noon-6pm; lunches $6-9.50). This modern café offers the usual range of coffee drinks, as well as smoothies and a changing menu of soups, sandwiches, and salads. Down the hill slightly and across the road is **Tai Wan Restaurant** (48 High St., 709/489-4222; Tues.-Sat. 11am-2:30pm and 4:30pm-10pm; $9-14), filled with bright red and gold furnishings and walls decorated in local art. The lunch and dinner buffets are $10 and $13, respectively.

Information

The **Visitor Information Centre** (709/489-6332, www.townofgrandfallswindsor.com; May-mid-Oct. daily 9am-9pm) is an old A-frame building along the TransCanada Highway on the west side of town.

Getting There

Grand Falls and Windsor are just shy of 100 kilometers (one hour) west of Gander via Route 1. From St. John's, it's a 430-kilometer, five-hour drive northwest on Route 1.

Deer Lake to Port-aux-Basques

It's 270 kilometers from the western hub of Deer Lake south to the ferry terminal at Port-aux-Basques. Along the way is Newfoundland's second-largest city, Corner Brook; Atlantic Canada's premier ski resort; and many interesting provincial parks and scenic detours.

DEER LAKE

Deer Lake, 640 kilometers west of St. John's and 270 kilometers from Port-aux-Basques, is a busy transportation hub at the point where Route 430 spurs north along the Northern Peninsula. The town lies at the north end of its namesake lake, a long body of water that flows into the Humber River. Along the lakeshore is a sandy beach and shallow stretch of water that offers pleasant swimming in July and August. The only commercial attraction is the **Newfoundland Insectarium** (2 Bonne Bay Rd., 709/635-4545; mid-May-mid-Oct. daily 9am-5pm, July-Aug. daily 9am-6pm; adult $12, senior $10, child $8). Inside this converted dairy, displays include active beehives and a collection of butterflies. To get there, take Exit 16 from the TransCanada

The Beothuks

Across the island's central area, the arrival of Europeans foretold grave consequences for the Beothuks, who had migrated from Labrador in AD 200 and spread across the Baie Verte Peninsula to Burnside, Twillingate, and the shores of the Exploits River and Red Indian Lake.

In 1769, a law prohibiting murder of the indigenous people was enacted, but the edict came too late. The Beothuks were almost extinct, and in 1819 a small group was ambushed by settlers near Red Indian Lake. In the ensuing struggle, a 23-year-old woman named Demasduit was captured, and her husband and newborn infant were killed. The government attempted to return her to her people when she contracted tuberculosis, but she was too ill, and she died in Botwood. In 1823, her kinswoman, Shanawdithit, was also taken by force. Shanawdithit told a moving tale of the history and demise of her people, punctuating it with drawings, maps, and a sampling of Beothuk vocabulary before she died in 1829, the last of her race.

You'll hear mention of the Beothuks throughout central Newfoundland, but two attractions concentrate on these almost mythical people—the **Beothuk Interpretation Site**, 70 kilometers north of Gander on the road to Twillingate, and Grand Falls' **Mary March Provincial Museum**, which is named for Demasduit's European given name.

Highway and follow Route 430 for a short distance to Bonne Bay Road.

Sir Richard Squires Provincial Park

Take Route 430 for eight kilometers to reach the turnoff to the remote Sir Richard Squires Provincial Park, which is then a further 47 kilometers from civilization. The park protects a short stretch of the upper reaches of the Humber River; salmon are the main draw. Even if you're not an angler, watching them leap up three-meter-high Big Falls in late summer makes the drive worthwhile. Camping is $15 per night.

Accommodations and Camping

Deer Lake Motel (15 TransCanada Hwy., 709/635-2108 or 800/563-2144, www.deerlakemotel.com; $110-140 s or d) is your typical low-slung roadside motel, but has regularly revamped rooms, a restaurant with dinner mains in the $14-24 range, and a small lounge.

Take the Nicholsville Road exit to reach Deer Lake RV Park (197 Nicholsville Rd., 709/635-5885, www.dlrvparkandcampground.com; late June-early Sept.; $24-29), close to the lake and with showers and a playground.

Information

Along the highway through town (beside the Irving gas station, with its big moose out front) is Deer Lake Information Centre (TransCanada Hwy., 709/635-2202; May-Oct. daily 8am-8pm), which has a number of displays on regional attractions and the Northern Peninsula.

Getting There

Deer Lake Airport (1 Airport Rd., 709-635-5270, www.deerlakeairport.com) is western Newfoundland's air hub. Located on the north side of town, just off the TransCanada Highway, it has Avis, Budget, Enterprise, Thrifty, and National car rental desks (make reservations well in advance). The airport is served by Air Canada (888/247-2262) from Halifax and Montréal, WestJet (888/937-8538) to Toronto, and Provincial Airlines (709/576-3943 or 800/563-2800, www.provincialairlines.ca) from throughout Newfoundland and Labrador.

Deer Lake is about 215 kilometers (2.5 hours) west of Grand Falls-Windsor on Route 1. From the ferry terminal in Port-aux-Basques, it's about 260 kilometers (three hours) north to Deer Lake on Route 1.

CORNER BROOK AND VICINITY

Corner Brook, 50 kilometers south of Deer Lake and 690 kilometers from the capital, lies at the head of the Humber Arm, 50 kilometers inland from the Gulf of St. Lawrence. The city is picturesquely cupped in a 20-square-kilometer bowl sloping down to the water, but most of the best natural attractions lie outside city limits, including the area around Marble Mountain and along Route 450 to Lark Harbour. The city ranks as Newfoundland's second largest, combining Corner Brook (pop. 20,000) with outlying settlements on the Humber Arm (another 20,000). It began as a company town, developing around a harbor-front pulp and paper mill that's still in operation, and has grown to become western Newfoundland's commercial, educational, service, and governmental center.

Town Sights

Making your way down to the harbor front from the TransCanada Highway is simple enough, but to visit the main downtown sights, orient yourself by stopping at the information center and deciding exactly what you want to see and do.

Captain Cook's Monument is a lofty lookout with views that provide a feeling for the layout of the city. On the road to the monument, you'll be rewarded with glorious views as far as the Bay of Islands. Follow O'Connell Drive across town, turn right (north) on Bliss Street, make another right on Country Road, turn left onto Atlantic Avenue with another

Corner Brook

O'CONNELL

COUNTRY RD

CARMEN

MAYFAIR AVE

ATLANTIC AVE

ASPEN RD

AVE

MT. BATTEN RD

DR

CARIBOU RD

WELLINGTON ST

VALLEY RD

HERALD AVE

MT BERNARD AVE

GARDEN HILL INN

CHURCHILL ST

ELIZABETH ST

UNIVERSITY DR

GREENWOOD INN & SUITES

MAIN ST

PARK ST

WEST ST

GLYNMILL INN

CORNER BROOK LIBRARY

COBB LN

Cobb Pond

CENTRAL ST

E. VALLEY RD

CORNER BROOK MUSEUM

HIGHER GROUNDS

LEWIN PKWY

PREMIER DR

HUMBER RD

CLARENCE ST

O'CONNELL DR

Margaret Bowater Park

WESTERN MEMORIAL REGIONAL HOSPITAL

BROOKFIELD AVE

W VALLEY RD

BLOMIDON GOLF AND COUNTRY CLUB

CONFEDERATION DR

MAMATEEK INN

MAPLE VALLEY RD

VISITOR INFORMATION CENTRE

COMFORT INN

To Stephenville and Port Aux Basques

STATION RD

To Marble Mountain and Deer Lake

CAPTAIN COOK'S MONUMENT

To Route 450

CURLING WATERFRONT RD

NEWFOUND SUSHI

LEWIN PKWY

Humber

Arm

Corner Brook Harbour

0   0.5 mi

0   0.5 km

left to Mayfair Street, and then right to Crow Hill Road. The monument itself commemorates Cook's Bay of Islands explorations with a plaque and sample chart.

In the wide bowl containing downtown, West Valley Road roughly divides the city in half. Near the bottom end of this thoroughfare and overlooking Remembrance Square is the staid Corner Brook Museum (2 West St., 709/634-2518; summer daily 9am-5pm, rest of the year Mon.-Fri. 9am-4:30pm; adult $5, child $3), housed in a historic building that has served as a post office, courthouse, and customs house through the years. Displays center around the various local industries and their impact on the city's growth.

Marble Mountain

Driving south from Deer Lake, you pass Marble Mountain (709/637-7601, www.ski-marble.com), 12 kilometers before reaching Corner Brook. The mountain rises from the east side of the highway, while on the other side of the road is the small community of Steady Brook, which fronts the Humber River. The resort is Atlantic Canada's largest and best-known alpine resort, and although the lifts don't operate in summer, the area is worth a stop during the warmer months. The highlight is Steady Brook Falls, accessible via a steepish trail that begins from the far corner of the main parking lot. The falls are reached in about 15 minutes. From there, a 3.5-kilometer (one-way) unmarked trail continues and brings you nearer to the peak. The views of the Humber Valley and Bay of Islands are splendid.

Between December and April, four chairlifts, including a high-speed detachable quad, whisk skiers from throughout Atlantic Canada and as far away as Toronto up 520 vertical meters to access 27 runs, a terrain park, and a half-pipe. The base area is dominated by a magnificent four-story, 6,400-square-meter day lodge, home to a ski and snowboard school, rental shop, café, restaurant, and bar. Lift tickets are adult $59, senior $43, child $32. Check the website for packages that include accommodations.

Route 450

This winding highway follows the south shore of Humber Arm for 50 kilometers, ending at the fishing village of Lark Harbour. From the TransCanada Highway, Route 450 begins at Exit 4 and bypasses the city; from downtown, take the Lewin Parkway west to reach Route 450. Rather than official attractions, this drive is worthwhile for its water-and-mountains scenery and picturesque fishing villages.

Almost at the end of the road is Blow Me Down Provincial Park. The park isn't extraordinarily windy, as the name might imply. Legend holds that a sea captain saw the mountain centuries ago and exclaimed, "Well, blow me down." The name stuck. From the park, sweeping views across the Bay of Islands make the drive worthwhile. You'll see the bay's fjord arms and the barren orange-brown Blow Me Down Mountains, as well as bald eagles and ospreys gliding on the updrafts, and perhaps caribou and moose roaming the preserve's terrain. The remote park has 28 campsites ($15), pit toilets, a lookout tower, and hiking trails.

Accommodations and Camping

CORNER BROOK

With the exception of the historic Glynmill Inn, Corner Brook motels serve casual highway travelers and those in town on business. A scenic alternative is to stay out at Marble Mountain.

Garden Hill Inn (2 Fords Rd., 709/634-1150 or 888/634-1150, www.gardenhillinn.ca; $95-120 s or d) offers nine nonsmoking rooms, each with private bath and TV, in an attractive clapboard house with a large garden. Breakfast is included, and guests also have the use of a kitchen.

The gracious Glynmill Inn (Cobb Ln., 709/634-5181 or 800/563-4400, www.steelehotels.com; from $130 s or d) hosts two restaurants and lies near the historic Townsite residential area. It's a charming inn banked with gardens of red geraniums. Rambling ivy, with leaves as large as maple leaves, covers the half-timber Tudor-style exterior. The wide front steps lead to an open porch, and the English-style foyer is furnished with wing chairs and sofas. All the rooms are comfortably furnished, but the older ones feature old-time spaciousness and antique marble in the bathroom.

Mamateek Inn (64 Maple Valley Rd., 709/639-8901 or 800/563-8600, www.mamateekinn.ca; from $115 s or d) is handy to the TransCanada Highway and has 55 adequate guest rooms, some with views down to Humber Arm. Rooms at the adjacent Comfort Inn (41 Maple Valley Rd., 709/639-1980 or 800/228-5150, www.choicehotels.ca; $120 s or d) are of a similar standard. Both inns have restaurants, the former with distant water views.

Greenwood Inn & Suites (48 West St., 709/634-5381 or 800/399-5381, www.greenwoodcornerbrook.com; from $150 s or d) is right downtown and across the road from Shez West, the best place in the city to sample Newfoundland cuisine. This full-service hostelry with regularly renovated guest rooms has its own English-style pub with sidewalk tables, an indoor heated pool, wireless Internet access, and underground parking.

MARBLE MOUNTAIN

Across the highway from Marble Mountain, 12 kilometers northeast of Corner Brook, is ★ Marble Inn (21 Dogwood Dr., Steady Brook, 709/634-2237 or 877/497-5673, www.marbleinn.com), a modern riverside complex that combines regular motel rooms (from $139 s or d) with luxurious two-bedroom suites overlooking the river ($289 s or d). Amenities include an indoor pool, a fitness room, spa services, a café, and a small restaurant open daily for dinner.

Also at Steady Brook is Marble Villa (709/637-7601 or 800/636-2725, www.skimarble.com; $139-249 s or d), which is right at the base of the alpine resort. Some units have separate bedrooms; all have cooking facilities and wireless Internet. Naturally, winter is high season, when most guests stay as part of a package. In summer, the self-contained units rent from $139 s or d.

George's Mountain Village (709/639-8168, www.georgesskiworld.com) has a limited number of campsites under the shadow of Marble Mountain. It's part of a complex that includes a restaurant, gas station, and sports shop. Powered sites are $35 and cabins with kitchens and separate bedrooms are $139 s or d.

Food

Beyond the fast-food places along all main arteries are some surprising dining options that require some searching out. Higher Grounds (9 Humber Rd., 709/639-1677; Mon.-Fri. 7am-10pm, Sat.-Sun. 9am-10pm; everything under $10) is an invitingly modern café with water views and free wireless Internet. Food is limited to soup and sandwiches, but the coffee and tea drinks are the best in town.

A real surprise in an otherwise unexceptional dining scene is ★ Newfound Sushi (117 Broadway, 709/634-6666; Mon.-Fri. 11am-8pm, Sat. noon-9pm; $12-24), away from the main street on the west side of downtown. The restaurant has just seven tables and a few seats along the sushi bar (or order take out), but the modern décor and local art is appealing, and it's the food itself that's the main draw—a wonderful array of sushi and sashimi that takes full advantage of local seafood such as salmon, crab, and shrimp. Order individually or try the Dory Load of Sushi for two. For non-sushi eaters, there are stir-fries.

The Glynmill Inn (Cobb Ln., 709/634-5181) has two restaurants. The more formal and intimate of the two is the downstairs Wine Cellar Steak House (Mon.-Sat. from 6pm; $24-35), a cozy setting with a fine wine list. This dining room serves up some of the city's best unadorned beef, including grilled filet mignon served in 12-ounce cuts. Upstairs beside the lobby, the more casual Carriage Room (daily 7am-2pm and 5pm-9pm; $13-30) specializes in Newfoundland fare with standard cooked breakfasts and then fried, poached, or broiled salmon, cod, halibut, and lobster the rest of the day.

Information and Services

Take Exit 5 or 6 from the TransCanada Highway and follow the signs to the Visitor Information Centre (11 Confederation Dr., 709/639-9792; daily Mon.-Fri. 8:30am-4:30pm, longer hours in summer), which is easily recognizable by its lighthouse-shaped design.

Western Memorial Regional Hospital (709/637-5000) is at 1 Brookfield Avenue. For the RCMP, call 709/637-4433.

Getting There and Around

Deer Lake, an hour's drive north of Corner Brook, has the region's main airport. DRL-LR (709/634-7422, www.drl-lr.com) operates bus service along the TransCanada Highway, with daily stops in Corner Brook (at the Confederation Dr. Irving gas station). Departures from St. John's at 8am arrive in Deer Lake at 5:15pm.

If you're coming up from the ferry at Port-aux-Basques, allow around two hours for the 210-kilometer trip north on Route 1. Corner Brook is 50 kilometers (1-hour drive) southwest of Deer Lake on Route 1.

The city has half a dozen cab companies whose cabs wait at lodgings, cruise business streets, and take calls. City Cabs (709/634-6565) is among the largest outfits.

STEPHENVILLE AND VICINITY

With a population of more than 8,000, Stephenville, 50 kilometers south of Corner Brook and then 40 kilometers west along Route 460, is the business hub for the Bay St. George-Port au Port region. In the center of town is Beavercraft (108 Main St., 709/643-4844), renowned for Winterhouse sweaters ($120-175), designed locally and produced by cottage-industry knitters. The shop is also a source for thrummed mittens ($20-30) and caps. This revived traditional craft combines a knitted woolen facing backed with raw fleece.

The shop shelves are stuffed with top-quality wares, including Woof Design sweaters, Random Island Weaving cotton placemats, King's Point Pottery platters and bowls, and handmade birch brooms.

Barachois Pond Provincial Park

One of western Newfoundland's most popular parks, 3,500-hectare Barachois Pond Provincial Park is beside Route 1 west of Stephenville. It is home to a 3.2-kilometer hiking trail through birch, spruce, and fir trees to Erin Mountain's barren summit (the trailhead is within the campground). Be on the lookout for the rare Newfoundland pine marten along the way. The view at the 340-meter summit extends over the Port au Port Peninsula. There's also a summertime interpretive program with guided walks and evening campfires, a lake for swimming and fishing, and 150 unserviced campsites ($15).

Accommodations

Stephenville offers a selection of downtown hotels and restaurants to travelers heading out onto the Port au Port Peninsula. The best of these is Dreamcatcher Lodge (14 Main St., 709/643-6655 or 888/373-2668, www.dreamcatcherlodge.ca; $99-129 s or d), at the far end of the main street through downtown. It comprises three buildings filled with a mix of motel rooms and kitchen-equipped units. The in-house restaurant is open Monday-Saturday 11am-9pm.

Getting There

Stephenville is 170 kilometers (two hours) north of Port-aux-Basques on Route 1.

STEPHENVILLE TO PORT-AUX-BASQUES

Most Northbound travelers, having just arrived in Newfoundland (and southbound travelers heading to the ferry) don't plan on lingering along the stretch of highway between Stephenville and Port-aux-Basques, but the detour into the Codroy Valley, 39 kilometers north of Port-aux-Basques, is worthwhile. Near the main highway is the Wetland Interpretation Centre (Route 406, Upper Ferry, 709/955-2109; June-Aug. daily 9am-5pm; free), where you can learn about the 300 bird species recorded in the valley, including great blue herons who are at the northern extent of their range. You can also ask for free bird checklists and a map showing the best viewing spots. Continue west to reach Codroy Valley Provincial Park, protecting a stretch of coastline including grass-covered sand dunes and a long sandy beach facing Cabot Strait. The highlight for birders will be the chance to spot shorebirds such as piping plovers (late spring to mid-summer).

Cape Anguille

Continue west beyond the provincial park along Route 406 to reach Cape Anguille, where ★ Cape Anguille Lighthouse Inn (Route 406, 709/634-2285 or 877/254-6586, www.linkumtours.com; May-Oct.; $100-110 s or d) sits high above a rugged shoreline. The lighthouse itself is still in use, but the lighthouse keeper (whose was born out here) has opened up a few simple rooms for guests in a trim red and white cottage adjacent to the main lighthouse. Breakfast is included, and a highly recommended dinner of local specialties ($30 per person) is available with advance notice.

Port-aux-Basques

Just over 900 kilometers from its starting point in St. John's, the TransCanada Highway reaches its western terminus at Port-aux-Basques, a town of about 5,000 with a deepwater port used by French, Basque, and Portuguese fishing fleets as early as the 1500s. Arriving in town from the north, the main highway continues two kilometers to the ferry terminal, and a side road branches west, past hotels and fast-food restaurants to the township proper. Here you'll find a cluster of commercial buildings along the harbor, including the Gulf Museum (118 Main St., 709/695-7560; July-Aug. daily 10am-8pm; $3). The highlights of this small museum are an astrolabe (a navigation aid dating to the early 1600s) and remnants from the SS *Caribou,* a ferry torpedoed by a German submarine as it crossed the Cabot Strait during World War II. Beyond the museum, turn left at the church and climb through a residential area to a lookout that affords 360-degree views of the town, the open ocean, and the ferry terminal.

sunset along the coast south of the Codroy Valley

ACCOMMODATIONS AND CAMPING

Just over two kilometers from the ferry terminal is Shark Cove Suites (16 Currie Ave., 709/695-3831; $90 s or d), a small complex of simple units. Each has a kitchen and a lounge with a TV/DVD combo. Originally a Holiday Inn, Hotel Port aux Basques (2 Grand Bay Rd., 709/695-2171 or 877/695-2171, www.hotel-port-aux-basques.com; $119-169 s or d) sits on the corner where the highway branches to the ferry terminal. The restaurant has a fair selection of local delicacies, and the hotel also has a lounge.

If you're camping, your best choice is six kilometers north of town, at J. T. Cheeseman Provincial Park, where more than 100 sites ($15-23) are spread along a picturesque stream. Facilities are limited, but the park is fronted by a long beach and is a nesting ground for the endangered piping plover.

INFORMATION

Housed in a distinctive pyramid-shaped building just north of the turnoff to town is a provincial Visitor Information Centre (709/695-2262; May-Oct. daily 9am-8pm and for all ferry arrivals).

GETTING THERE

Port-aux-Basques is 165 kilometers (two hours) south of Stephenville via Route 1.

CONTINUING TO THE MAINLAND BY FERRY

Port-aux-Basques is the northern terminus of year-round Marine Atlantic (709/227-2431 or 800/341-7981, www.marine-atlantic.ca) ferry service from North Sydney (Nova Scotia). It's the shorter and less expensive of the two crossings to Newfoundland from North Sydney. One-way fares and rates for the five- to seven-hour sailing are adult $44, senior $40, child $20, vehicle under 20 feet $114. Extras include reserved chairs in a private lounge ($23) and cabins ($130-170).

Gros Morne National Park

UNESCO World Heritage Sites are scattered across the world. Egypt boasts the pyramids. France is known for Chartres Cathedral. Australia has the Great Barrier Reef. And Newfoundland boasts 1,085-square-kilometer Gros Morne National Park, a spectacular geological slice of the ancient world.

Gros Morne is on Newfoundland's west coast, 72 kilometers northwest from the town of Deer Lake. While the geological history will amaze you, there's also a wealth of hiking and boating tours and cross-country skiing in winter. Even though the park is remote, it is surrounded by small towns that cater to visitors, with lodging and restaurants to suit all budgets. There's even a dinner theater.

The Land

The park fronts the Gulf of St. Lawrence on a coastal plain rimmed with 70 kilometers of coast, edging sandy and cobblestone beaches, sea stacks, caves, forests, peat bogs, and breathtaking saltwater and freshwater fjords. The flattened Long Range Mountains, part of the ancient Appalachian Mountains, rise as an alpine plateau cloaked with black and white spruce, balsam fir, white birch, and stunted tuckamore thickets. Bare patches of peridotite, toxic to most plants, speckle the peaks, and at the highest elevations, the vegetation gives way to lichen, moss, and dwarf willow and birch on the arctic tundra.

Innumerable moose, arctic hares, foxes, weasels, lynx, and a few bears roam the park. Two large herds of woodland caribou inhabit the mountains and migrate to the coastal plain during winter. Bald eagles, ospreys, common and arctic terns, great black-backed

Gros Morne National Park

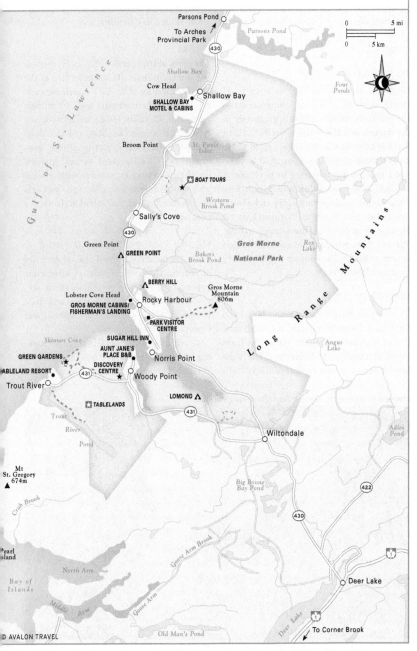

Parsons Pond
To Arches
Provincial Park
430

Parsons Pond

0 ___ 5 mi
0 ___ 5 km

Shallow Bay

Four
Ponds

Cow Head
Shallow Bay
**SHALLOW BAY
MOTEL & CABINS**

Gulf of St. Lawrence

Broom Point
St. Pauls
Inlet

⭐ **BOAT TOURS**

Western
Brook Pond

Sally's Cove
430

Green Point
△ **GREEN POINT**

Bakers
Brook Pond

*Gros Morne
National Park*

Rex
Lake

△ **BERRY HILL**

Gros Morne
Mountain
806m ▲

Lobster Cove Head
**GROS MORNE CABINS/
FISHERMAN'S LANDING**

Rocky Harbour

■ **PARK VISITOR
CENTRE**

Long Range Mountains

Angus
Lake

Skinner Cove

SUGAR HILL INN

**AUNT JANE'S
PLACE B&B**

GREEN GARDENS ★

**DISCOVERY
CENTRE** ★

Norris Point

ABLELAND RESORT
Trout River
431
Woody Point

⭐ **TABLELANDS**

Trout
River
Pond

△ **LOMOND**

431

Wiltondale

Adies
Pond

Mt
St. Gregory
674m ▲

Crab Brook

Big Bonne
Bay Pond

422

430

earl
land

North Arm

Goose Arm Brook

To Corner Brook

Bay of
Islands

Middle Arm

Goose Arm

Old Man's Pond

Deer Lake

Deer Lake

© AVALON TRAVEL

gulls, and songbirds nest along the coast, while rock ptarmigans inhabit the mountain peaks. You might see willow ptarmigans on the lower slopes or, especially during the June to early July capelin run, a few pilot, minke, or humpback whales offshore.

Park Entry

Gros Morne National Park is open year-round, although all but one campground and the two information centers operate only in the warmer months. A National Parks Day Pass is adult $10, senior $8.50, child $5, to a maximum of $20 per vehicle. It is valid until 4pm the day following its purchase. A Viking Trail Pass (adult $45, senior $36, child $24) is valid for park entry and admission to Northern Peninsula National Historic Sites for seven days from the date of purchase. Passes can be purchased at the information center at Rocky Harbour or the Discovery Centre at Woody Point.

ROUTE 430

This is the main route up the Northern Peninsula. From Wiltondale, it's 86 kilometers to the park's northern extremity; from Rocky Harbour, it's 51 kilometers. The highway traverses terrain typical of the island's rocky seacoast and verdant hills and mountains, a distinct contrast to the southern area. Unusual groups of faulted and folded rock layers lie along this coastline.

Lobster Cove Head

The point of land north of Rocky Harbour is Lobster Cove Head. Its layers formed as the North American plate slid beneath the eastern Eurasian/African plate 450-500 million years ago. Exhibits inside Lobster Cove Head Lighthouse (late May-mid-Oct. daily 10am-5:30pm; free) depict local lore, geological facts, and ancient natural history, but the views from outside are what make a visit worthwhile, especially as the sun sets over Bonne Bay and the Gulf of St. Lawrence beyond.

Rocky Harbour to Cow Head

More dramatically formed coastal rock lies farther north. Green Point, 17 kilometers beyond Lobster Cove, presents a tilted, textured surface of ribbon limestone and shale embedded with fossils from the Cambrian and Ordovician Periods.

Continuing north, you'll come to the parking lot for the short trail to Western Brook Pond. One kilometer farther is where Western

Moose are common throughout Gros Morne National Park.

From Wiltondale, 31 kilometers north of Deer Lake, Route 431 leads west, entering the park after 13 kilometers.

Discovery Centre

If you've entered Gros Morne on Route 431, make your first stop the Discovery Centre (709/458-2417; mid-May-June and Sept.-early Oct. daily 9am-5pm, July-Aug. daily 9am-6pm; included in park entry fee), on the hill above Woody Point. This modern facility showcases everything the national park is renowned for. The main display area holds an impressive 3-D map of the park, geological samples and descriptions, a human history display, and a theater. A gift shop sells park literature, and a café specializes in regional cuisine. Outside, a short trail leads through a garden planted with species native to the park.

★ Tablelands

The Tablelands, the park's most prized geological tract, lies along Route 431, halfway between Woody Point and Trout River. It's an odd sight, more resembling Hudson Bay's bleached brown barrens than verdant Newfoundland. The 12-by-7-kilometer chunk once lay beneath the ancient Iapetus Ocean. Violent internal upheavals eventually thrust the unearthly landscape to the surface. The parched yellow and tan cliffs and boulders that resulted are formed of peridotite, an igneous rock found in the Earth's mantle. You can get a good idea of the landscape from the parking lot, but I encourage you to take a stroll along the easy Tablelands Trail. It's four kilometers each way, but you only need walk a short way to get a feeling for the starkness of the moonlike terrain.

Trout River

After leaving the Tablelands behind, Route 431 descends to the small fishing village of Trout River, on a protected bay 18 kilometers from Woody Point. A boardwalk rims the stony beach, leading past weather-worn

Lobster Cove Head Lighthouse

Brook drains into the Gulf of St. Lawrence. You'll find a sandy beach and an oceanfront picnic area. The headland immediately to the north is Broom Point. Along the access road is a platform and telescope, which you can train on the mountains that rise from Western Brook Pond.

Cow Head

Cow Head, 10 kilometers north of Broom Point, features an angled formation similar to that of Green Point, with limestone breccia (jumbled limestone chunks and fossils) spread across a small peninsula. The areas are richly textured. At Cow Head, the breccia looks like light-colored rock pillows scattered across a dark rock surface, while Green Point's surface is a rich green and textured like crushed velvet. The rock layers at both places originated during deepwater avalanches as the Iapetus Ocean formed 460-550 million years ago. In the village itself, beside St. Mary's Church, is a small botanical garden.

wooden buildings to the mouth of the Trout River, where wharves are filled with lobster pots and fishing gear. Fronting the boardwalk are historic buildings open to the public, including the bright-yellow 1898 Jacob A. Crocker House. Across the river, turn right over the bridge and look for a small sign on the left. This marks the start of a short trail (10 minutes round-trip) leading to the Old Man, a rock stack that is visible from town.

RECREATION

More than 100 kilometers of marked and unmarked hiking trails lead novice to expert trekkers into the park's nooks and crannies. Several privately operated boat tours probe the fjords. A provincial fishing license (available at any sports store) opens up angling for brook trout and arctic char on the fast-flowing streams and rivers.

If you'd like to know more about Gros Morne's natural history and geology, plan on attending a scheduled interpretive program and evening campfire talk; see the information center for a schedule.

Hiking

Even if you're not a keen hiker, you can enjoy short interpretive walks at Broom Point (32

kilometers north of Rocky Harbour) and the Tablelands, as well as the two-kilometer circuit of Lobster Cove Head. If you're planning on taking a boat tour on Western Brook Pond, you'll need to lace up your hiking boots for the three-kilometer walk to the dock. But it's the following two longer hikes that get most of the attention.

Between the Tablelands and Trout River are two trailheads for the Green Gardens. This feature originated as lava from erupting volcanoes in the Iapetus Ocean. The hike has two trailheads. The longer option (16 kilometers round-trip; allow six hours) begins from Route 431 on the west side of the Tablelands. Four kilometers farther west is another trailhead for the Green Gardens. This is a nine-kilometer loop (four hours). Regardless of which trail you take, the trails emerge on a high headland cloaked in rich green grasses overlooking the gulf. Below the headland, sea stacks and sea caves (accessible only at low tide) rise from the beach floor beside cliffs pocked with pillow lava, the solidified remnants of molten rock from 100 kilometers beneath the ancient seafloor.

Feeling fit? If so, the hike to the 806-meter bald summit of Gros Morne Mountain (eight kilometers one-way; allow eight hours

the moonlike Tablelands

The Galápagos of Geology

"What the Galápagos are to biology, Gros Morne is to geology," declared Britain's Prince Edward when he visited and dedicated Gros Morne National Park as a UNESCO World Heritage Site in 1987.

Long before Newfoundland was an island, it was a landlocked part of a great supercontinent formed during Precambrian times. When the supercontinent broke apart, the land plates drifted, and a rift formed that filled with water—the Iapetus Ocean. After another 50 million years, give or take, the land plates reversed direction and moved toward each other. As the landmasses were pushed together, Newfoundland, not yet an island, perched high and dry near the center of another supercontinent. At that point, Newfoundland's only distinctive characteristic was a mountain rib—the budding Appalachian Mountains that now rim North America's eastern edge.

Strewn among the mountains now protected by Gros Morne National Park was a colossal geological heritage: remnants from the world's first supercontinent and parts of the Iapetus Ocean's seafloor. East of the mountains, the island's central plateau portion was made up of a great rectangular swatch of the crumpled ancient seabed, 200-250 kilometers in width and length.

Between then and now, the eons added a few more topographical touches. The retreating ice sheet uncovered the Labrador Trough, scooped out the Strait of Belle Isle, cut fjords into the coastlines, and pocked the interiors to create myriad lakes, such as spectacular Western Brook Pond.

for the round-trip) may be what you're looking for. Beginning from Route 430, just east of the main information center, the first hour's walking is across flat terrain. Tightly packed boulders mark the beginning of the actual ascent, which takes 2-2.5 hours. Unexpectedly, the trail empties at a corner of the flattened peak. The air is clear and exhilarating, but surprisingly chilly. Far below, climbers scramble fitfully up the rocky ascent. To the west rise the Long Range Mountains. Looking south, you'll see a sapphire fjord, laid like an angled ribbon across the green woodlands. The summit is bare shale, limestone, and quartzite rock sprinkled with wild grass tufts. Check weather forecasts before heading out, and carry raingear, a first-aid kit, and extra food, clothing, and drinking water. If you're not entirely comfortable undertaking this hike by yourself, consider joining a group organized by Gros Morne Adventures (709/458-2722 or 800/685-4624, www.grosmorneadventures.com), which charges $125 per person for a day hike.

★ Boat Tours

Like Scandinavia, Gros Morne National Park is famous for fjords, fringed sea arms carved by the last ice sheet and shouldered by forests and cliffs. Unlike their Scandinavian counterparts, the most spectacular are actually landlocked fjord lakes and are known as "ponds." These ponds—Trout River, Ten Mile, Bakers Brook, and Western Brook—were carved by the ice sheets. But in each case, when the enormous ice sheet melted out, the coastline—which had been compressed by the sheer weight of the glacier—rebounded like a sponge, rising above sea level and cutting the fjord off from the sea.

Bontours (709/458-2016 or 888/458-2016; adult $56-65, child $20-25.50) offers a cruise on spectacular Western Brook Pond. Tickets can be booked by phone or in person at the Ocean View Motel in Rocky Harbour. To get to Western Brook Pond, you must drive 30 kilometers north from Rocky Harbour to a marked parking lot. From this point, it's a three-kilometer hike to the boat dock. During July and August, three tours depart daily (10am, 1pm, and 4pm), while in June and September there's just one tour daily (1pm). Plan on leaving Rocky Harbour at least 90 minutes before the scheduled departure time. This tour lasts two hours.

Other Tours
Gros Morne Adventures (709/458-2722

or 800/685-4624, www.grosmorneadventures.com) leads geology and natural-history tours through the park from June through September. The six-day backpacking adventure on the Long Range Traverse costs $1,295, inclusive of meals, permits, and camping accommodations. Kayaking is another specialty; a half-day with instructions costs $115 per person, an overnight trip is $345, and kayak rentals from the company's Norris Point base cost $50-60 per day.

ENTERTAINMENT AND EVENTS

To immerse yourself in the culture of Newfoundland, plan on spending an evening at the Gros Morne Theatre Festival (709/639-7238, www.theatrenewfoundland.com), which runs June through mid-September at Cow Head, 48 kilometers north of Rocky Harbour. The festival comprises two plays enacted by more than 40 professional actors, with performances that tell the story of people and events that have helped shape the province. Tickets cost adult $30-45, child $18-25.

In Rocky Harbour, the Anchor Pub (Ocean View Hotel, Main St., 709/458-2730; daily 11:30am-close) has traditional Newfoundland music Monday, Wednesday, and Friday nights through summer. The cover charge is minimal, and it gets surprisingly crowded.

ACCOMMODATIONS

Rocky Harbour, 72 kilometers from Deer Lake, has the best choice of accommodations and is centrally located for exploring the park.

Rocky Harbour

Those not camping will find a variety of accommodations in Rocky Harbour, the park's major service area. For B&B accommodations, Evergreen B&B (4 Evergreen Ln., 709/458-2692 or 800/905-3494; $85 s, $95 d) has three guest rooms and a large patio with barbecue facilities. It's open year-round, and rates include a full breakfast.

The Ocean View Hotel (Main St., 709/458-2730 or 800/563-9887, www.theoceanview.ca; mid-March-mid-Dec.; from $149-269 s or d) enjoys a prime location across from the water in the heart of Rocky Harbour. Rooms in the older wing are high-quality and spacious, while those in the newer wing offer ocean views (from $169). The motel also has a downstairs bar with nightly entertainment, an upstairs restaurant, a booking desk for Western Brook Pond boat tours, and a super-funky old-fashioned elevator.

A short walk from the harbor, the units at Mountain Range Cottages (32 Parsons Ln., 709/458-2199, www.mountainrangecottages.com; mid-May-mid-Oct.; $120-150 s or d) are an excellent value. Each of 10 simple but modern cottages has a full kitchen, a dining table, two separate bedrooms, a bathroom, and a balcony equipped with outdoor furniture and a barbecue.

Continue around the southern side of Rocky Harbour to reach ★ Gros Morne Cabins (Main St., 709/458-2020 or 888/603-2020, www.grosmornecabins.com; $130-190 s or d), a modern complex of 22 polished log cabins strung out along the bay. Unfortunately, they don't take full advantage of the wonderful location (small windows and no balconies), but each has a kitchen, separate bedrooms, a propane barbeque, and wireless Internet. Other amenities include a playground and laundry, while part of the complex is a large general store.

Cow Head

In Cow Head, 48 kilometers north of Rocky Harbour, Shallow Bay Motel and Cabins (193 Main St., 709/243-2471 or 800/563-1946, www.shallowbaymotel.com; $90-130 s or d) lies close to long stretches of sandy beach, hiking trails, and Arches Provincial Park. The 66 guest rooms are basic but comfortable, and the 20 cabins have full kitchens. Amenities include a large restaurant and one of the only outdoor pools in western Newfoundland (don't worry, it's heated!).

Along Route 431

A luxurious lodging that seems a little out of place within this remote national park, Sugar Hill Inn (115 Sexton Rd., Norris Point, 709/458-2147 or 888/299-2147, www.sugarhillinn.nf.ca; $165-255 s or d) is nevertheless a treat. The 11 guest rooms are accentuated with polished hardwood floors and earthy yet contemporary color schemes. The King Suite has a vaulted ceiling, jetted tub, and sitting area with a leather couch. Breakfast is included in the rates, while dinner (mains $28-38) is extra. The inn is on the left as you descend to Norris Point.

One block back from the water in the heart of the village of Woody Point is Aunt Jane's B&B (1 Water St., 709/453-2485, www.grosmorneescapes.com; mid-May-mid-Oct.; $65-85 s or d), a charming 1880s home that contains five guest rooms, four with shared bathrooms. Aunt Jane's is one of numerous other guest houses in town collectively marketed as Victorian Manor Heritage Properties (same contact). One of these is Uncle Steve's, a trim three-bedroom home with a kitchen and a TV lounge. It costs $225 per night, with a three-night minimum.

Trout River

At the end of Route 431 and a 10-minute walk along the river from the ocean, Tableland Resort (709/451-2101, www.tablelandresortandtours.com; May-Oct.; $130 s or d) has seven two-bedroom cottages, a restaurant, and a laundry.

CAMPING

Almost 300 campsites at five campgrounds lie within Gros Morne National Park. No electrical hookups are available, but each campground has flush toilets, fire pits (firewood costs $8 per bundle), at least one kitchen shelter, and a playground. All campgrounds except Green Point have hot showers.

A percentage of sites at all but Green Point can be reserved through Parks Canada

(877/737-3783, www.pccamping.ca) for $11 per reservation—reassuring if you're visiting the park in the height of summer. The remaining sites fill on a first-come, first-served basis.

Route 430

Across Route 430 from Rocky Harbour, Berry Hill Campground (mid-June-early Sept.; $19-26) has 69 sites, showers, kitchen shelters, and a playground. It fills quickly each summer afternoon, mostly with campers that have made advance reservations through Parks Canada, but also because of its central location.

The 31-site ★ Green Point Campground ($16), 12 kilometers north of Rocky Harbour, is the only park campground open year-round, and it is the only one without showers. The oceanfront setting more than makes up for a lack of facilities.

At the park's northern extremity, Shallow Bay Campground (early June-mid-Sept.; $19-26) offers full facilities and 62 sites within walking distance of the services of a small town.

Route 431

Lomond Campground (mid-May-early Oct.; $19-26) edges Bonne Bay's east arm. It is popular with anglers but also is the start of three short walking trails, including one along the Lomond River.

Turn left at the end of Route 431 to reach Trout River Pond Campground (early June-mid-Sept.; $19-26), which is close to the Trout River boat tour dock. It's only a small facility (44 sites), but it has a beautiful setting, hot showers, a playground, and wireless Internet.

FOOD
Rocky Harbour

If you rise early, head to ★ Fisherman's Landing (44 Main St., 709/458-2060; daily 6am-11pm; $11-21), across from the wharf, for a cooked breakfast special that includes juice and coffee. The rest of the day, it's traditional

Newfoundland cooking at reasonable prices—grilled pork chops with baked potatoes and boiled vegetables, poached halibut, pan-fried cod tongues, and more. House wine is sold by the glass, but some bottles are under $25. A few tables have water views.

Cow Bay

Part of the Shallow Bay Motel complex, the Bay View Family Restaurant (193 Main St., 709/243-2471; daily 7am-9pm; $11-24) does indeed have bay views, but only from a few of the tables. Dining choices are as simple as a Newfie Mug (tea and molasses bread), but you can also order more recognizable meals, such as blackened salmon with Cajun spices and T-bone steaks.

Woody Point

The Lighthouse Restaurant (39 Water St., 709/453-2213; daily 11am-8pm; $12-18) has simple seafood meals, including the park's best fish-and-chips, a poached cod dinner, and deep-fried scallops. It's across from the waterfront.

Trout River

Along the waterfront in this end-of-the-road fishing village, the Seaside Restaurant (709/451-3461; mid-May-mid-Oct. daily noon-10pm; $12-24) enjoys sweeping water views. The restaurant has a reputation for consistently good food. The seafood chowder is overflowing with goodies, and fish-and-chips are cooked to perfection.

INFORMATION AND SERVICES

The Park Visitor Centre (Rte. 430, 709/458-2417; mid-May-June and early Sept.-mid-Oct. daily 9am-5pm, July-early Sept. daily 8am-8pm) stocks literature, sells field guides, presents slide shows, and has exhibits on the park's geology, landscapes, and history. Outside is a telescope for a close-up view of Gros Morne Mountain. The center is along Route 430, just before the turnoff to Rocky Harbour.

The Discovery Centre (Route 431, 709/458-2417; mid-May-June and Sept.-early Oct. daily 9am-5pm, July-Aug. daily 9am-6pm) is another source of park information. For pre-trip planning, go to the Parks Canada website (www.pc.gc.ca) or check out the business links at www.grosmorne.com.

GETTING THERE AND AROUND

The nearest airport is in Deer Lake, 72 kilometers from Rocky Harbour. It is served by Air Canada (888/247-2262) from Halifax and Montréal. Rental car companies with airport desks include Avis, Budget, Enterprise, National, and Thrifty. Each allows 200 free kilometers per day, meaning you'll be unlikely to rack up extra charges on a trip to the park.

To get to Rocky Harbour from Deer Lake, head north on Route 430 for 70 kilometers (50 minutes). From the ferry terminal in Port-aux-Basques, it's about 340 kilometers (four hours) north to Rocky Harbour via Route 1 and Route 430.

Northern Peninsula

North of Gros Morne National Park, the Northern Peninsula sweeps northeast across mountainous, flat-topped barrens and ends in tundra strewn with glacial boulders. Route 430 (also known as the Viking Trail) runs alongside the gulf on the coastal plain and extends the peninsula's full length, finishing at St. Anthony, 450 kilometers north of Deer Lake.

As you drive this stretch of highway, you'll notice, depending on the time of year, either small black patches of dirt or tiny flourishing vegetable gardens lining the road. These roadside gardens belong to the people of the nearby villages; because of the region's nutrient-poor soil, people plant their gardens wherever they find a patch of fertile ground.

NORTH FROM GROS MORNE

Arches Provincial Park

Right beside the highway, just north of Gros Morne National Park, the intriguing geological feature known as Arches Provincial Park is well worth the drive, even if you're not planning on traveling up the Northern Peninsula. Two arches have been eroded into a grassed rock stack that sits along the rocky beach. At low tide you can climb underneath, but most visitors are happy to stand back and snap a picture.

Daniel's Harbour

About 15 kilometers north of Arches Provincial Park is the village of Daniel's Harbour. It has an interesting little harbor and historic buildings such as Nurse Myra Bennett Heritage House, once home to a woman known throughout Newfoundland and Labrador as the "Florence Nightingale of the North" for her medical exploits.

On the south side of town is Bennett Lodge (Rte. 430, 709/898-2211, www.bennettlodge.com; May-Oct.; $85-95 s or d), nothing more than a modular motel with a restaurant and dimly lit lounge. But it's one of the least expensive motels on the Northern Peninsula and has ocean views through the small guest room windows.

PORT AU CHOIX

About 160 kilometers north of Rocky Harbour, a road spurs west off Route 430 for 10 kilometers to Port au Choix, a small fishing village with a human history that dates back more than 4,500 years. The historic site related to these early residents is the town's main attraction, but the local economy revolves around the ocean and cold-water shrimp (those tasty little shrimp you see in salads and the like).

Port au Choix National Historic Site

The Maritime Archaic people and the later Dorset and Groswater Inuit migrated from Labrador, roamed the Northern Peninsula, and then settled on the remote cape beyond the modern-day town of Port au Choix. Today, the entire peninsula is protected, with trails leading to the various dig sites. Start your exploration of the Port au Choix National Historic Site at the Visitor Reception Centre (709/861-3522; mid-June-mid-Sept. daily 9am-5pm; adult $8, senior $6.60, child $4), which is signposted through town. Here, the three cultures are represented by artifacts, exhibits, and a reconstruction of a Dorset Inuit dwelling. Dig sites are scattered over the peninsula, with a 3.5-kilometer trail leading from the center to the most interesting site, Phillip's Garden. First discovered in the 1960s, archaeological digs here revealed Dorset dwellings and an incredible wealth of Maritime Archaic cultural artifacts buried with almost 100 bodies at three nearby burial grounds. The digs continue to this day, and through summer you can watch archaeologists doing their painstaking work (if you're lucky, you may even see them uncover an ancient artifact). Free guided hikes depart daily at 1pm. If you drive through town beyond the shrimp-processing plant, you pass an Archaic cemetery and a parking lot (from which Phillip's Garden is a little closer, 2.5 kilometers one-way).

Museum of Whales and Things

Along the main road into town, the small Museum of Whales and Things (709/861-3280; Mon.-Sat. 9am-5pm; donation) is the work of local Ben Ploughman, who has, as the name suggests, collected a 15-meter-long sperm whale skeleton, as well as other "things." In an adjacent studio, Ploughman makes and sells driftwood creations.

Accommodations

As the town of Port au Choix continues to

unfold its rich archaeological heritage, it also continues to expand its visitor services. One of these is **Jeannie's Sunrise Bed and Breakfast** (84 Fisher St., 709/861-2254 or 877/639-2789, www.jeanniessunrisebb.com; $99-120 s or d), owned by lifelong Port au Choix resident Jeannie Billard. Each of the six rooms is bright and spacious and has its own TV. The less expensive rooms share a bathroom. Rates include a full breakfast, and dinner is available on request.

Sea Echo Motel (Fisher St., 709/861-3777, www.seaechomotel.ca; $94 s, $110-140 d) has 30 fairly standard motel rooms with wireless Internet, three cabins, a restaurant with lots of local seafood, and a lounge.

Food

As you cruise through town, it's difficult to miss the ★ **Anchor Café** (Fisher St., 709/861-3665; summer daily 9am-11pm, spring and fall daily 10am-10pm; $6.50-17), with its white ship's bow jutting out into the parking lot. With the cold-water shrimp plant across the road, this is the place to try the local delicacy ($6 for a shrimp burger). You can also eat like locals have done for generations (corned fish with sides of brewis, pork scrunchions, and a slice of molasses bread) or try a Moratorium Dinner (a reference to the cod-fishing ban), such as roast turkey. Also good is the cod and shrimp chowder.

Along the same road, the **Sea Echo Motel** (Fisher St., 709/861-3777; daily 7am-9pm; $14-24) has a nautically themed restaurant with similar fare, including fish cakes and cod tongues.

Getting There

Port au Choix is 160 kilometers (two hours) north of Rocky Harbour on Route 430. From the ferry terminal in Port-aux-Basques, it's 700 kilometers (six hours) driving north along Route 1 and Route 430 to Port au Choix.

PLUM POINT

At Plum Point, 60 kilometers north of Port au Choix, Route 430 continues north and Route 432 spurs east toward Roddickton. The latter is the longer route to St. Anthony, but an abundance of moose makes it an interesting alternative.

Bird Cove

Although visited by Captain Cook in 1764 and settled permanently by Europeans in 1900, Plum Point's first residents made a home for themselves as early as 4,500 years ago. These Maritime Archaic people were prehistoric hunters and gatherers who spent summers on the edge of **Bird Cove**. The two adjacent village sites, discovered as recently as the 1990s, were rare because they presented archaeologists with an undisturbed look at life many thousands of years ago. Shell middens, spear points used to hunt sea mammals, and tools used for woodworking have all been excavated. A boardwalk with interpretive panels leads around the site. To get there, drive to the end of the road, loop left past the grocery store, and take the unpaved road on the right-hand side of the light brown house. The boardwalk is on the left, a little under one kilometer from the grocery store.

Dog Peninsula

Beyond the general store, stay right as the road loops around, and you soon find yourself at a bridge linking the **Dog Peninsula** to the mainland. The peninsula is laced with walking trails that follow the shoreline and pass through the remains of an 1880s settlement. You can complete the first loop (turn right at the far end of the bridge) in around 30 minutes, even with time spent skimming a few of the super-flat stones into Bird Cove.

Accommodations and Food

Out on the highway, the **Plum Point Motel** (709/247-2533 or 888/663-2533, www.

plumpointmotel.com; $110-120 s or d) has 40 motel rooms and 18 basic cabins with kitchenettes. With a few water-view tables, the in-house restaurant (daily 7am-9pm; $10-21) serves the usual array of cooked breakfasts, included salted cod, tea, and toast.

Getting There

Plum Point is about 60 kilometers (50 minutes) north of Port au Choix via Route 430. From the ferry terminal in Port-aux-Basques, it's about 550 kilometers (6.5-7 hours) north to Plum Point via Route 1 and Route 430.

ST. BARBE

St. Barbe, 30 kilometers north of Plum Point and 300 kilometers north of Deer Lake, is where ferries depart for Labrador. There's little to see or do in town, but accommodations are provided at the **Dockside Motel** (709/877-2444 or 877/677-2444, www.docksidemotel.nf.ca; $89-129 s or d), which isn't at the dock at all. Instead, it's on the road leading down to the waterfront. Rooms are basic but adequate, and the simple in-house restaurant is open daily for breakfast, lunch, and dinner.

Getting There

St. Barbe is 20 kilometers (20 minutes) north of Plum Point via Route 430. From the ferry terminal in Port-aux-Basques, it's 570 kilometers (seven hours) north to St. Barbe via Route 1 and Route 430.

Catching the Ferry to Labrador

If you are planning on exploring the Labrador Straits region, make ferry reservations long before arriving in St. Barbe. The ticket office is at the Dockside Motel, and even with reservations, you'll need to check in before heading down to the dock. The ferry **MV Apollo** (866/535-2567, www.labradormarine.com) sails from St. Barbe once or twice daily between early May and early January. The

crossing takes around two hours. The one-way fare is a reasonable vehicle and driver $25, extra adult $8, senior and child $6.60. Across the road from the Dockside Motel is a fenced compound with hookups for RVs and a drop-off area for those catching the ferry and not wanting to travel with full rigs.

ST. BARBE TO ST. ANTHONY

It's 110 kilometers between St. Barbe and St. Anthony. For the first 50 kilometers, Route 430 hugs the Strait of Belle Isle, passing a string of fishing villages clinging tenuously to the rocky coastline. Tourist services are minimal, but there are a couple of worthwhile stops, and you should take the time to wander through one or more of these outports to get a feeling for the sights, sounds, and smells that go with living along this remote stretch of coastline.

Deep Cove Wintering Interpretation Site

Just beyond the turnoff to the modern-day village of Anchor Cove is **Deep Cove Wintering Interpretation Site,** an observation platform and trail that leads to the site of an 1860s village where residents of Anchor Cove would spend the winter. Only the weathered remains of a few wooden homes are left, but the site is interesting as one of the rare cases of European seasonal migration. It takes about 10 minutes to reach the site from Route 430.

★ Thrombolites of Flowers Cove

The picturesque village of **Flowers Cove,** its low profile of trim homes broken only by the occasional church spire, lies 13 kilometers north of St. Barbe. Turn onto Burns Road from Route 430 to reach the red-roofed Marjorie Bridge. Beyond the bridge, a boardwalk leads along the cove to an outcrop of thrombolites. Resembling flower-shaped boulders, they are actually the remnants of algae and bacteria that have been dated at 650 million years old, making them among the earliest forms of life on earth. While the actual thrombolites are, of course, interesting, it is the complete lack of surrounding hype for what is one of the world's rarest fossils (the only other place they occur is on the remote west coast of Australia) that makes visiting the site even more unforgettable.

ST. ANTHONY

Although you will want to continue north to L'Anse aux Meadows, St. Anthony (pop. 2,400), 450 kilometers north of Deer Lake, is the last real town and a service center for the entire Northern Peninsula. Most attractions revolve around Dr. Wilfred Grenfell, a medical missionary from England who established hospitals along both sides of Labrador Straits in the late 1800s. His impact on St. Anthony was especially powerful. It was here, in 1900, that Grenfell built his first year-round hospital and established a medical mission headquarters. St. Anthony still serves as the center of operations for the International Grenfell Association, which continues to build hospitals and orphanages and funds other community endeavors across the country.

The main natural attraction is Fishing Point Park, through town. From this lofty point, you have the chance to spy whales or icebergs.

Grenfell Historic Properties

Start your discovery of everything Grenfell at the Grenfell Interpretation Centre (West St., 709/454-4010; July-Aug. daily 8am-5pm, Sept.-June Mon.-Fri. 8am-5pm; adult $10, senior $8, child $3). This large facility details Grenfell's many and varied accomplishments, from the establishment of his first hospital at Battle Harbour to the work of the association that carries his name today. Grenfell also helped foster financial independence for remote outports through profitable organizations such as Grenfell Handicrafts, which

The thrombolites of Flowers Cove are the world's oldest living organisms.

still produces hand-embroidered cassocks, fox-trimmed parkas, hooked rugs, and jackets that are sold at a gift shop across from the admissions desk of the Grenfell Interpretation Centre.

Exit the museum through the tearoom and you come across the tiny Dock House Museum (July-Aug. daily 10am-4pm; free). Displays here describe how Grenfell's ships were pulled from the water for repairs after long voyages to remote communities.

A tribute to the life and works of Dr. Grenfell lives in the Jordi Bonet Murals, impressive ceramic panels adorning the walls of the rotunda at the entrance to Curtis Memorial Hospital, which is across the road from the Grenfell Interpretation Centre.

Exhibits at the stately green and white Grenfell House Museum (July-Aug. daily 8am-5pm, Sept.-June Mon.-Fri. 8am-5pm; free entry with proof of paid admission to Interpretation Centre July-Aug. daily 8am-5pm, Sept.-June Mon.-Fri. 8am-5pm), his home for many years, describe Grenfell's home and family life. The home is on the far side of the hospital, a five-minute walk from the Interpretation Centre. A trail starting from behind the home leads to Tea House Hill, where viewing platforms provide sweeping harbor views.

Tours

As the gateway to Iceberg Alley, St. Anthony is the place to take to the water in a tour boat. **Northland Discovery** (709/454-3092 or 877/632-3747; late May-mid-Sept., adult $58, child $25) departs three times daily from behind the Grenfell Interpretation Centre. When there's a lack of icebergs (mid-June through August is the best viewing period), the captain concentrates on searching out humpback, minke, and fin whales, as well as seabirds. The covered vessel is stable and has washrooms. The 2.5-hour tours include hot drinks.

Accommodations

Fishing Point B&B (Fishing Point Rd., 709/454-3117 or 866/454-2009; from $90 s or d) is through town and within walking distance of Lightkeeper's, the best place to eat in town. Built in the 1940s, the converted fisherman's home is set right on the harbor and has three guest rooms with either private or en suite bathrooms. Rates include a full breakfast.

Haven Inn (14 Goose Cove Rd., 709/454-9100 or 877/428-3646, www.haveninn.ca; $103-145 s or d) has 30 rooms in various configurations on a slight rise off Route 430. Rooms are fairly standard, but each has a coffeemaker and hair dryer; the more expensive ones have water views and gas fireplaces. The in-house restaurant dishes up inexpensive breakfasts.

Grenfell Heritage Hotel (1 McChada Dr., 709/454-8395 or 888/450-8398, www.grenfellheritagehotel.ca; $130-170 s or d) is the town's newest lodging, but it's also the most expensive. Rooms are simple but clean and comfortable. Kitchenettes, a free continental breakfast, and handy waterfront location are all pluses.

Food

Drive through town to reach ★ **Lightkeeper's** (Fishing Point Rd., 709/454-4900; summer daily 11:30am-9pm; $16-32), which, true to its name, follows a red-and-white color scheme that extends all the way down to the salt and pepper shakers. Housed in a converted light-keeper's residence overlooking the ocean (you may spot icebergs June through August), this tiered dining room is casual, although a little on the expensive side. Starters include crab claws with garlic butter while mains are mostly from the ocean, including seafood.

Haven Inn (14 Goose Cove Rd., 709/454-9100; daily 7am-9pm; $13-18) has a small bright dining room that catches the morning sun. Cooked breakfasts are $8.

Getting There

It's 115 kilometers (1.5 hours) from St. Barbe to St. Anthony going east on Route 430. From the ferry terminal in Port-aux-Basques, it's about 680 kilometers (9.5 hours) north to St. Anthony via Route 1 and Route 430.

★ L'ANSE AUX MEADOWS

At the very end of Route 436 lies L'Anse aux Meadows, 48 kilometers from St. Anthony and as far as you can drive up the Northern Peninsula. It was here that the Vikings came ashore more than 1,000 years ago—the first Europeans to step foot in North America. Two Viking attractions make the drive worthwhile, but there's also a fine restaurant and lots of wild and rugged scenery.

L'Anse aux Meadows National Historic Site

Long before archaeologists arrived, Newfoundlanders were aware of the odd-shaped sod-covered ridges across the coastal plain at L'Anse aux Meadows. George Decker, a local fisherman, led Norwegian scholar-explorer Helge Ingstad and his wife, archaeologist Anne Stine Ingstad, to the area in the 1960s. The subsequent digs uncovered eight

L'Anse aux Meadows National Historic Site

complexes of rudimentary houses, workshops with fireplaces, and a trove of artifacts, which verified the Norse presence. National recognition and site protection followed, leading to the creation of the L'Anse aux Meadows National Historic Site in 1977 and to UNESCO designating it a World Heritage Site the following year.

A Visitor Reception Centre (Rte. 436, 709/623-2608; June-early Oct. daily 9am-5pm, July and Aug. until 6pm; adult $12, senior $10, child $6) has been developed above the site. Here, you can admire excavated artifacts, view site models, and take in an audiovisual presentation. A gravel path and boardwalk lead across the grassy plain to the site of the settlement, where panels describe the original uses of buildings now marked by depressions in the grass-covered field. Just beyond is a settlement of re-created buildings overlooking Epaves Bay. Costumed interpreters reenact the roles and work of the Norse captain, his wife, and four crew members.

Norstead

Just beyond the turnoff to L'Anse aux Meadows National Historic Site is Norstead

(Rte. 436, 709/623-2828; mid-June-mid-Sept. daily 9am-6pm; adult $10, senior $8, child $6.50), the re-creation of a Viking port of trade. Aside from the Viking theme, it has little resemblance to how the Vikings of L'Anse aux Meadows lived, but it is still well worth visiting. Right on the water, you can see a full-size replica of a Viking ship, listen to stories in the dimly lit Chieftains Hall, watch a blacksmith at work, and sample bread as it comes from the oven in the dining hall. The costumed interpreters bring this place to life, and you can easily spend an hour or more listening and watching them at work and play.

Accommodations and Camping

The village of L'Anse aux Meadows comprises just a smattering of homes on the headland. For overnight accommodations, there are a few choices back toward St. Anthony, all more enjoyable than staying in one of St. Anthony's nondescript motels.

The closest accommodations are in Hay Cove, a cluster of houses two kilometers before the end of the road. Stay in one of five comfortable guest rooms at Jenny's Runestone

House (709/623-2811 or 877/865-3958, www. jennysrunestonehouse.ca; April-Oct.; $80-90 s or d) and enjoy a hot breakfast each morning. Also in Hay Cove, **Viking Village Bed and Breakfast** (709/623-2238 or 877/858-2238, www.vikingvillage.ca; $62 s, $78 d) has five en suite guest rooms, ocean views, a TV room, and laundry facilities.

The units at **Southwest Pond Cabins** (Rte. 436, Griquet, 709/623-2140 or 800/515-2261, www.southwestpondcabins.ca; May-Oct.; $99 s or d) overlook a small lake nine kilometers from L'Anse aux Meadows. Each of 10 spacious wooden cabins has a kitchen, separate bedrooms, satellite TV, and a bathroom. Other amenities include a playground, barbecues, and a grocery store. Excellent value.

At the top of the list for originality is ★ **Quirpon Lighthouse Inn** (Quirpon Island, 709/634-2285 or 877/254-6586, www. linkumtours.com; May-Oct., $250-275 s, $350-375 d), a converted light-keeper's residence and modern addition that house a total of 11 guest rooms, each with an en suite. Rates include all meals and boat transfers (45 minutes) from Quirpon. To get to Quirpon, turn off Route 436, six kilometers beyond Griquet. Watch icebergs float by and whales frolick in the surrounding waters, or join a Zodiac tour searching out whales and icebergs ($50 extra per person).

One of the few commercial campgrounds this far north is **Viking RV Park** (Rte. 436, Quirpon, 709/623-2425; June-Sept.), where tent campers pay $20 and RVs wanting hookups are charged $26 per night.

Food

Amazingly, at the end of the road is one of the finest dining rooms in all of Newfoundland, the ★ **Norseman Restaurant** (709/754-3105; late May-late Sept. daily noon-9pm; $19-38). Admittedly, the ocean views add to the appeal, but the food is fresh and creative, the service professional, and the setting casual yet refined. Starters include a smooth shellfish-less seafood chowder, smoked char, and lots of salads. Ordering lobster takes a little more effort than usual—you'll be invited to wander across the road with your waitress to pick one from an ocean pound. Other entrées include cod baked in a mustard and garlic crust and grilled Labrador caribou brushed with a red-wine glaze. Still hungry? It's hard to go past a slice of freshly baked pie filled with local berries.

The ★ **Dark Tickle Company** (75 Main St., Griquet, 709/623-2354; June-Sept. daily

Quirpon Lighthouse Inn

9am-6pm, Oct.-May Mon.-Fri. 9am-5pm) uses locally harvested berries to create a delicious array of jams, preserves, sauces, and even chocolates and wines. You can watch the various processes in creating the finished product, but you'll also want to sample and purchase them from the attached store.

Getting There

It's 40 kilometers (40 minutes) north from St. Anthony to L'Anse aux Meadows via Route 430 and Route 436. From the ferry terminal in Port-aux-Basques, it's 700 kilometers (10 hours) north to L'Anse aux Meadows via Route 1, Route 430, and Route 436.

RALEIGH

Between St. Anthony and L'Anse aux Meadows, Route 437 branches off Route 436 to the delightfully named Ha Ha Bay and the small town of Raleigh.

★ Burnt Cape Ecological Reserve

Encompassing a barren landscape of limestone, the Burnt Cape Ecological Reserve is an unheralded highlight of the Northern Peninsula. The plant life is especially notable, as many species would normally only be found in Arctic regions, while others, such as Long's Braya and Burnt Cape cinquefoil, are found nowhere else in the world. A geological oddity are *polygons,* circular patterns of small stones formed by heavy frosts. On the western edge of the cape are sea caves, some big enough to hold pools of water when the tide recedes. Looking straight ahead from the parking lot, you'll see aquamarine pools of water at the base of the cliffs, known locally as the Cannon Holes. The sun reflecting on the limestone bedrock warms the trapped seawater, and you'll often see locals taking a dip on hot days.

To get there, turn left in downtown Raleigh, round the head of Ha Ha Bay, and follow the rough unpaved road up and through the barrens. The end of the road is a semi-official parking lot high above the ocean, four kilometers from the interpretive board at the entrance to the reserve. As there are no marked trails and many of the highlights are hidden from view, stop by the office at Pisolet Bay Provincial Park (just before Raleigh, 709/454-7570) for directions and up to date information on access.

Accommodations and Camping

The only accommodation in town is a good one—Burnt Cape Cabins (709/452-3521, www.burntcape.com; $109-129 s or d), which are beside a café (daily 8am-9pm) serving inexpensive seafood and lobster dinners. Each of the seven modern cabins has a TV, Internet access, and comfortable beds, or choose to rent the affiliated three-bedroom home.

Just before Route 437 descends to Raleigh, it passes Pisolet Bay Provincial Park (709/454-7570; June-mid-Sept.; $15), which offers 30 sites, a kitchen shelter, washrooms with showers, and a lake with a beach and swimming for the brave.

Getting There

To get to Raleigh from St. Anthony, it's 30 kilometers (25 minutes) north via Route 430 and Route 437. From the ferry terminal in Port-aux-Basques, it's 690 kilometers (10 hours) north to Raleigh via Route 1, Route 430, and Route 437.

Labrador

Look for ★ to find recommended
sights, activities, dining, and lodging.

Highlights

★ **L'Anse Amour:** North America's oldest known burial site and an imposing stone lighthouse combine to make the short detour to the "cove of love" a highlight (page 84).

★ **Red Bay National Historic Site:** Four Spanish galleons lie in Red Bay; onshore displays tell their story and that of what was at one time the world's largest whaling port (page 86).

★ **Battle Harbour:** Known locally as "outports," dozens of remote communities throughout Newfoundland and Labrador have been abandoned over the last few decades. Battle Harbour is one of the few that encourages tourism (page 86).

★ **North West River:** A short drive from Happy Valley-Goose Bay, this small community is home to the Labrador Interpretation Centre, while down along the river you can watch local Innu hauling in the day's catch (page 89).

★ **Torngat Mountains National Park:** This remote park can only be reached by charter flight, but once there, adventurous visitors can explore the mountains on foot and the coastline by kayak (page 95).

S panning 294,330 square kilometers, two and a half times the size of Newfoundland island and three times the size of the three Maritime provinces, Labrador dominates Atlantic Canada. This, the mainland portion of Newfoundland

and Labrador, resembles an irregular wedge pointing toward the North Pole, bordered on the east by 8,000 kilometers of coastline on the Labrador Sea, and on the west and south by the remote outskirts of Québec. Thorfinn Karlsefni, one of several Norse explorers who sailed the coastline around AD 1000, is said to have dubbed the region "Helluland" for the large flat rocks, and "Markland" for the woodlands. Jacques Cartier described the coastline as a "land of stone and rocks" during a 1534 voyage.

Labrador can be divided into three geographical destinations. Along the Strait of Belle Isle—the narrow passage between Labrador and Newfoundland—is a string of communities fronting the strait. Known as the Labrador Straits and linked to Newfoundland by ferry, this region was a Basque whaling center in the 1500s. Modern sightseers have rediscovered the strait and its archaeological treasures at Red Bay and L'Anse Amour.

Spruce forests, interspersed with bogs and birch and tamarack stands, dominate the wilderness of central Labrador. The watery complex of Lobstick Lake, Smallwood Reservoir, Michikamau Lake, and the Churchill River and its tributaries are the main geographical features. The Churchill flows out of the western saucer-shaped plateau and rushes eastward, widening into Lake Melville at the commercial hub of Happy Valley-Goose Bay, which grew from an important military base. In western Labrador, iron-ore mining developed in the late 1950s. The twin cities of Labrador City and Wabush started as mining towns, and together they now serve as the region's economic and transportation center. With a population of 11,300, Labrador City/Wabush is Labrador's largest municipality. Between Labrador City and Happy Valley-Goose Bay, a massive hydroelectric plant, developed in the late 1960s, spawned another company town—Churchill Falls. Linked to

---

Labrador

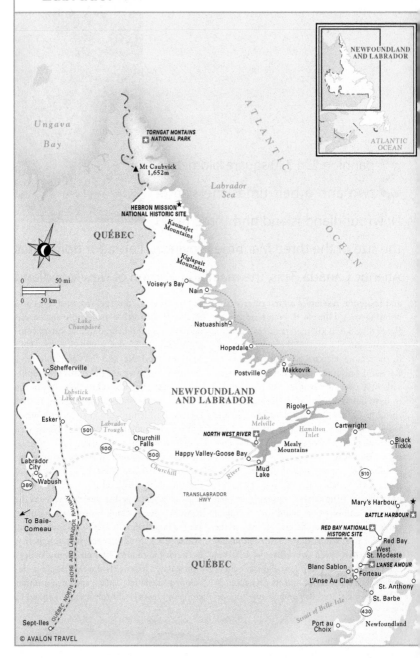

the outside world by ferry, the North Coast is dotted with tiny Inuit settlements within the Nunatsiavut land claim area.

Many visitors to Labrador are anglers, who rank the sportfishing here among the world's best. And the fishing is said to be Atlantic Canada's finest as well: It's not uncommon to land an *ouananiche* (landlocked salmon) weighing four kilograms. Brook trout here range 3-4 kilograms, lake trout to 18 kilograms, northern pike 9-14 kilograms, and arctic char 5-7 kilograms.

PLANNING YOUR TIME

Because of its remote location, Labrador is the least-visited region of Atlantic Canada. It can be divided into three regions—Labrador Straits, across the Strait of Belle Isle from Newfoundland's Northern Peninsula; Central Labrador, along the TransLabrador Highway; and the North Coast. While the northern regions attract serious adventurers, the main attractions lie along the Labrador Straits, easily accessible by ferry from the Northern Peninsula, where along a 120-kilometer stretch of highway is a string of picturesque fishing villages. Some are more historic than others. At L'Anse Amour, you can view North America's oldest known burial site; Red Bay National Historic Site tells the story of a Basque whaling port. One of the most moving experiences in all of Atlantic Canada is a visit to Battle Harbour, an island fishing community that was abandoned in the late 1960s. Today, you can relive the glory days of this remote port, and even stay overnight. Unlike many other destinations, getting to and traveling around Labrador is part of the adventure, and nothing is more "out there" than exploring the remote wilderness of Torngat Mountains National Park.

Getting around Labrador requires some advance planning. The communities of Labrador Straits are linked by Route 510 from Blanc Sablon, where ferries land from Newfoundland. The 510 extends north from Port Hope Simpson for 370 kilometers through Cartwright Junction to Happy Valley-Goose Bay. From Happy Valley-Goose Bay, it's 520 kilometers west to Labrador City.

Deciding *when* to travel to Labrador is easy. July and August are the only two months during which you'll find all attractions open. June and September are shoulder months,

LABRADOR

hiking in the Torngat Mountains

when the weather is a little cooler and attractions begin opening and closing. Also be aware that transportation is conducted on a weather-permitting basis. Early-season ice packs and late-season storms can delay the ferries. The region's smaller aircraft need daylight and good visibility. An absence of both may ground flights for days.

Labrador Straits

The communities of Labrador Straits lie across the Strait of Belle Isle from Newfoundland. They are linked by a 160-kilometer stretch of paved road that extends between Blanc Sablon (Québec) and Mary's Harbour. From Mary's Harbour, an unpaved road loops inland and continues north to Goose Bay.

Getting There by Ferry

The ferry MV *Apollo* (866/535-2567, www. labradormarine.com; one-way vehicle and driver $25, extra adult $8, senior and child $6.60) links the Labrador Straits to Newfoundland. Ferries depart St. Barbe, 300 kilometers north of Deer Lake, once or twice daily between early May and early January. The crossing takes around two hours. The arrival point is Blanc Sablon, located in Québec but just a five-minute drive from L'Anse-au-Clair, within Labrador. If the weather is pleasant, find a spot outside and keep an eye out for whales. Inside are a café and gift shop. Reservations are not required but are definitely recommended for travel in July and August. Even with a reservation, upon arrival at St. Barbe you should check in at the ferry office. It is within the Dockside Motel (on the right before the terminal) and opens two hours before scheduled departures. At Blanc Sablon, the ferry office is at the terminal, along with a craft shop, food concession, and information booth.

L'ANSE-AU-CLAIR

Founded in the early 18th century by French sealers, L'Anse-au-Clair is the closest strait community to the Québec border. Fishing is still the livelihood for the population of about 300, although crafts also contribute to the economy. For these, head to Moore's Handicrafts (8 Country Rd., 709/931-2086; June-Sept. Mon.-Sat. 9am-9pm), signposted across from the information center. Pieces to look for include hand-knit woolens, winter coats, cassocks, and moccasins.

Sights and Recreation

The Gateway to Labrador Visitor Centre (38 Main Hwy., 709/931-2013, www.labrador-coastaldrive.com; mid-June-Sept. daily 9am-6pm), the region's interpretive center, seen as you enter town from Québec, is in a handsomely restored, early-20th-century Anglican church. Inside, exhibits, photographs, fossils,

ferry from St. Barbe to the Labrador Straits

Gateway to Labrador Visitor Centre

7am-10pm; $14-28) is well-priced throughout the day, with dinner mains topping out at $28 for steamed crab legs with mashed potato and vegetables. Other dinner offerings are as simple as spaghetti and meatballs and as fishy as pan-fried halibut.

FORTEAU

Established as a cod-fishing settlement by islanders from Jersey and Guernsey in the late 1700s, Forteau remains a fishing community, not only in the cod industry but also as a base for anglers fishing the salmon- and trout-filled Forteau and Pinware Rivers.

The Bakeapple Folk Festival, held over three days in mid-August, is always popular. The gathering includes traditional music, dance, storytelling, crafts, and Labrador foods.

Accommodations and Food

Forteau's accommodations include the Grenfell Louie A Hall Bed and Breakfast (3 Willow Ave., 709/931-2916, www.grenfell-bandb.ca; May-Sept.; $80 s, $90 d including breakfast), in a nursing station built by the International Grenfell Association. The five guest rooms are comfortable but share bathrooms. Other amenities include an antique-filled dining room and a lounge where you can watch films on the Grenfell legacy or read up on local history.

Along the highway in the center of town, Seaview Restaurant and Cabins (33 Main St., 709/931-2840 or 866/931-2840, www.labradorseaview.ca; $100-110 s or d) has motel rooms, not cabins, but they are comfortable, and each has one or two bedrooms, a kitchen, and wireless Internet. The restaurant (daily 9am-10pm; $12-24) has a few local specialties, including caribou baked in a juniper sauce, and lots of dishes using locally caught fish.

Getting There

Forteau is 10 kilometers east of L'Anse au Clair via Route 510.

and artifacts represent the area's fishing heritage.

The information center staff can also point out two interesting walks. The shorter of the two is to the "Jersey Rooms," site of an early-1700s sealing station operated by men from Jersey. Only stone foundations and a stone walkway remain, but the two-kilometer trail also offers sweeping ocean views. The trailhead is signposted beyond the wharf. At the far end of the beach, a trail leads across the barrens to Square Cove, where the boilers are all that remain of a 1954 shipwreck. In August, wild strawberries are a bonus along this three-kilometer (each way) walk.

Accommodations and Food

The largest accommodation along the Labrador Straits is the Northern Light Inn (58 Main St., 709/931-2332 or 800/563-3188, www.northernlightinn.com; $109-159 s or d), which has 54 comfortable rooms and a few RV sites ($25). The inn's restaurant (daily

The Grenfell Legend

Labrador's harsh living conditions and lack of medical care attracted Dr. Wilfred Grenfell, the British physician-missionary. Dr. Grenfell worked with the Royal National Mission to Deep Sea Fishermen on the North Sea. A visit in 1892 convinced him that serving the people of remote Labrador and northern Newfoundland was his calling. He established Labrador's first coastal hospital at Battle Harbour the next year, followed by a large mission at St. Anthony. From the mission, he sailed along the coast in boats, treating 15,000 patients in 1900 alone. By 1907 he had opened treatment centers at Indian Harbour, Forteau, North West River, and seven other remote settlements. For his efforts, he was knighted.

Dr. Grenfell initiated a policy of free medical treatment, clothing, or food in exchange for labor or goods. Funded by private contributions and the Newfoundland government, he opened cooperative stores, nursing homes, orphanages, mobile libraries, and lumber mills. He also initiated the Grenfell Handicrafts programs and home gardening projects. In 1912, he formed the International Grenfell Association to consolidate the English, Canadian, and American branches that funded his work. The physician was subsequently knighted a second time, in 1927, and also awarded recognition by the Royal Scottish Geographical Society and other notable organizations.

★ L'ANSE AMOUR

Just off Route 510, this tiny community comprises just four houses, all owned by members of the Davis family, residents since the 1850s. The bay was originally named Anse aux Morts ("Cove of the Dead") for the many shipwrecks that occurred in the treacherous waters offshore. A mistranslation by later English settlers resulted quite charmingly in the name L'Anse Amour ("Cove of Love").

Maritime Archaic Burial Mound National Historic Site

Turn off Route 510 to L'Anse Amour and watch for a small interpretive board on the right, which marks the Maritime Archaic Burial Mound National Historic Site. Here, in 1973, archaeologists uncovered a Maritime Archaic burial site of a 12-year-old boy dated to 6900 BC, which makes it North America's oldest known funeral monument.

the village of L'Anse Amour

The dead boy was wrapped in skins and birch bark and placed face-down a pit. Items such as a walrus tusk were excavated from the pit, and other evidence points to a ceremonial feast. The artifacts found here are on display at The Rooms in St. John's.

Point Amour Lighthouse

At the end of the road is Point Amour Lighthouse (709/927-5825; mid-May-early Oct. daily 9:30am-5pm; adult $6, senior $4, child $3). The strait's rich sea has attracted intrepid fishing fleets through the centuries: The early Basques sailed galleons into Red Bay, followed by English and French fleets, and eventually Newfoundlanders arrived in schooners to these shores. By 1857, shipwrecks littered the treacherous shoals, and the colonial government erected this 33-meter-high beacon, Atlantic Canada's tallest. Now restored, the stone lighthouse and light-keeper's residence (now the interpretive center) feature displays and exhibits on the history of those who have plied the strait's waters. The 122-step climb to the top (the final section is a ladder) affords excellent views of the strait and the surrounding land.

Accommodations

One of the village's four homes operates as

★ Lighthouse Cove B&B (709/927-5690; $50 s, $60 d), with three rooms open year-round for travelers. The hosts, Rita and Cecil Davis, are very hospitable, spending the evening with guests relating stories of the area and their family's long association with the cove. When you make a reservation, be sure to reserve a spot at the dinner table (extra) for a full meal of traditional Labrador cooking, using game such as moose and caribou. Breakfast, included in the rate, comes with homemade preserves.

Getting There

L'Anse Amour is 12 kilometers east of Forteau on Route 510.

RED BAY

Little evidence is left today, but 400 years ago, Red Bay was the world's largest whaling port. Not discovered until the 1970s, four Spanish galleons at the bottom of the bay have taught archaeologists many secrets about the whaling industry and early boat construction; an excellent historic site here brings the port to life. The village itself, 40 kilometers north of L'Anse Amour, has limited services.

It is estimated that between 1540 and 1610, around 2,500 Basque men (from an area of

Point Amour Lighthouse

Spain near the French border) made the crossing from Europe each year, traveling in up to 30 galleons that returned to Europe filled with whale oil. The Basques came to harvest right whales, which migrated through the Strait of Belle Isle. Most of the men lived aboard the galleons, but evidence shows that some built simple shelters on the mainland and Saddle Island, where red roof tiles still litter the beaches.

★ Red Bay
National Historic Site

Four Spanish galleons lie in Red Bay, including the well-preserved *San Juan.* Archaeologists have done extensive research on all four, and they now lie in the cold shallow water covered with tarpaulins. While you can't view the actual boats, two excellent facilities combine to make up Red Bay National Historic Site (709/920-2051; June-late Sept. daily 9am-5pm; adult $8, senior $6.50, child $4). Coming off the highway, the first of the two site buildings is a modern structure centering on a *chalupa,* another wooden whaling boat recovered from the bottom of Red Bay. You can watch a documentary on the galleon *San Juan* and have staff point out where each of the galleons is located. Keep your receipt and head toward the waterfront, where the main collection of artifacts is held. Displays describe how the four galleons, each from a different era, have helped archaeologists track ship design through the 16th and 17th centuries. Highlights include a scale model of the *San Juan,* pottery, and remains of a compass and sandglass.

Accommodations and Food

The single lodging choice at Red Bay is Basin View B&B (Rte. 510, 709/920-2002; $55-75 s or d, includes a light breakfast), a modern home overlooking the bay from a rocky shoreline just before reaching the town itself. The three downstairs rooms share a single bathroom. The upstairs guest room has a private bathroom but less privacy, as it is on the main level of the house.

Down by the harbor but without water views, Whaling Station Restaurant (709/920-2060; daily 8am-9pm; $9-15) is one of the region's better dining rooms. The seafood chowder is good, as is the beef soup. For a main, the fish-and-chips is delicious, while the pork chop dinner is simple and hearty.

Getting There

Red Bay is 60 kilometers (one hour) north of L'Anse Amour via Route 510.

MARY'S HARBOUR

Beyond Red Bay, Route 510 is unpaved for 80 kilometers to Mary's Harbour. This small fishing village, where the local economy revolves around a crab-processing plant, was isolated until 2000, when the road was completed.

The main reason to travel this far north is to visit Battle Harbour, and since the ferry leaves from Mary's Harbour, the local Riverlodge Hotel (709/921-6948, www.riverlodgehotel.ca; $100-110 s or d) makes a sensible overnight stop. The 15 rooms are simple but comfortable, and the in-house restaurant has pleasant views across the St. Mary's River.

Getting There

Mary's Harbour is about 90 kilometers (one hour) north of Red Bay via Route 510.

★ BATTLE HARBOUR

On a small island an hour's boat ride from Mary's Harbour lies Battle Harbour, a remote yet intriguing outport village that is well worth the effort to reach.

Established as a fishing village in 1759, it was one of the earliest European settlements on the Labrador coast. By 1775, Battle Harbour's cod-fishing industry had made the settlement the economic center of the region, a status that faded and then rebounded a century later with the arrival of seasonal fishers from Newfoundland. By 1848 Battle Harbour was the capital of Labrador, an important trade and supply center where up to 100 vessels would be tied up in port at any one time. Thanks to the work of missionary Wilfred Grenfell, the residents had year-round medical services and, by 1904, state-of-the-art communications thanks to the Marconi Wireless Telegraph Company, which erected a station here in 1904.

In the late 1960s, with the inshore fishery in decline, Battle Harbour residents were re-settled on the mainland at Mary's Harbour, leaving the community an abandoned out-port. A few local families continued to spend summers on the island, but it wasn't until 1990 that the Battle Harbour Historic Trust took over the site and began an ambitious restoration program that continues to this day. Now protected as a national historic site, Battle Harbour allows a glimpse into the past. About 20 structures have been restored, including an Anglican church, the original mercantile salt fish premises, the loft from which Robert Peary told the world of his successful expedition to reach the North Pole, a general store, and a massive fish "flake" (drying platform). A boardwalk links many of the restored buildings, tapering off near the back of the village, where a dozen or so homes stand in varying states of disrepair and a trail leads through a rock cleft to a cemetery.

Accommodations and Food

In addition to restoring many of the most important buildings, the **Battle Harbour Historic Trust** (709/921-6325, www.battleharbour.com) does a wonderful job of providing visitor services, including accommodations, meals, and transportation.

On a rise overlooking the town and Great Caribou Island, a merchant's home has been converted to the ★ **Battle Harbour Inn** (709/921-6325, www.battleharbour.com; $250-265 pp/night including island transfers and meals). Three of the five guest rooms have double beds; two have single beds. Other buildings with beds include the hostel-style Cookhouse; the Grenfell Doctor's Cottage, which has harbor views; the Constable Forward Cottage; the three-bedroom Isaac Smith Cottage, which is lighted by oil lamps and heated by wood fire; and the very private two-bedroom Spearing Cottage. Check the website for package pricing.

Meals are provided in a dining room above the general store. All are hearty, with plenty of cross-table conversation between diners. At the general store itself, you can buy snacks and basic provisions.

Battle Harbour

Getting There and Around

The trip between Mary's Harbour and Battle Harbour takes around one hour aboard a small enclosed ferry (inn guests only). The ferry departs Mary's Harbour daily at 11am, and the return trip departs Battle Harbour at 9am. The ferry transfer is included in all overnight packages. Once on the island, all lodging is within easy walking distance of the ferry dock.

CARTWRIGHT

Most travelers incorporate Cartwright into their itineraries as part of a loop that includes driving the TransLabrador Highway through to Happy Valley-Goose Bay.

From Mary's Harbour, it is 167 kilometers to Cartwright Junction (no services), from where the TransLabrador Highway continues around the Mealy Mountains to Happy Valley-Goose Bay; Cartwright is 87 kilometers north along Route 516.

Sights

The town was named for 18th-century merchant adventurer and coastal resident Captain George Cartwright; Flagstaff Hill Monument, overlooking the town and Sandwich Bay, still has the cannons Cartwright installed to guard the harbor 200 years ago.

Gannet Islands Ecological Reserve, off the coast, is a breeding colony for common murres, puffins, black-legged kittiwakes, and the province's largest razorbill population. North of Cartwright lies the spot where Norse sailors first laid eyes on the coast: Wunderstrands, a magnificent 56-kilometer stretch of sandy golden beach across Sandwich Bay that is only accessible by boat. The local tour operator, Experience Labrador (709/653-2244 or 877/938-7444, www.experiencelabrador.com), offers sea kayaking day trips, but you're missing the local highlight if you simply paddle around local waterways and don't take a day trip to the Wunderstrand. Now protected as part of Mealy Mountains National Park, the beach was named by infamous Viking Erik the Red and still to this day receives few visitors. The cost is $250 s, $300 d for the six-hour adventure, booked through Experience Labrador.

Accommodations and Food

In 2013, the town's only accommodation, the Cartwright Hotel (3 Airport Rd., 709/938-7414, www.cartwrighthotel.ca) burnt to the ground. As of press time, the owners plan on rebuilding, so check their website for updates.

Getting There

Cartwright is about 250 kilometers (3.5 hours) north of Mary's Harbour via Route 530.

Central Labrador

HAPPY VALLEY-GOOSE BAY

Happy Valley-Goose Bay (pop. 7,500) spreads across a sandy peninsula bordered by the Churchill River, Goose Bay, and Terrington Basin at the head of Lake Melville. Although remote, it is linked to the outside world by the TransLabrador Highway (Churchill Falls is 288 kilometers to the west and 620 kilometers southeast to Blanc Sablon) and scheduled air services.

During World War II, Canadian forces selected the Goose Bay site and, with assistance from the British Air Ministry and the U.S. Air Force, built a massive airbase and two airstrips there. Before the war ended, 24,000 aircraft set down for refueling during the transatlantic crossing. Currently operated by the Canadian Armed Forces, 5 Wing Goose Bay Airport serves as a training center for Canadian, British, Dutch, Italian, and German air forces, since the latter four countries have no airspace of their own suitable for low-level flight training. Goose Bay

Happy Valley-Goose Bay

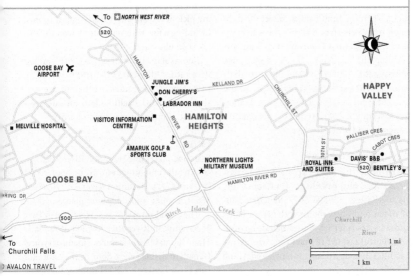

is also an important refueling stop for transatlantic flights, with a runway long enough to accommodate space shuttle landings in an emergency. The town last hit the headlines on September 11, 2001, when the airport filled with commercial flights that were diverted from their intended destinations.

Happy Valley-Goose Bay originally evolved as two distinct areas: Goose Bay, rimming an important air base, and adjacent Happy Valley, which became the base's residential and commercial sector. In 1961 the two areas joined as Happy Valley-Goose Bay and elected the first town council, which was Labrador's first municipal government. The distinction between the two areas remains firm, so be prepared to consult a map as you wander around. Goose Bay connects to Happy Valley by the L-shaped Hamilton River Road, the main drag.

Town Sights

In the Northern Lights Building, the **Northern Lights Military Museum** (170 Hamilton River Rd., 709/896-5939; Tues.-Sat. 9am-5:30pm; free) offers exhibits pertaining to military history from World War I to the Vietnam War. Displays include uniforms, medals, documents, weapons, and photographs. Across the hall, the **Trapper's Brook Animal Display** exhibits stuffed native animals and birds—from beavers and bears to bald eagles. Also in the building is the **Labrador Institute** (709/896-6210), an arm of Memorial University of Newfoundland. Of interest to the public is an archive of historic maps and photographs, along with a crafts display.

★ North West River

This community of 500, 38 kilometers northeast of Goose Bay on Route 520, was the center of the area until the 1940s. The settlement began as a French trading post in 1743, and the inhabitants are descendants of French, English, and Scottish settlers.

Within town are two worthwhile sights. The **Labrador Interpretation Centre** (2 Portage Rd., 709/497-8566; early May-Sept. Mon.-Sat. 9am-4:30pm, Sun. noon-4:30pm; free) is filled with interesting exhibits that catalog the natural and human history of "the

Big Land." Beyond the center, Portage Road leads to piers and pleasant views. If you'd like to meet some of the locals, arrive in late afternoon, when the Innu fishers collect the day's catch from nets strung across the waterway. Within an original Hudson's Bay Company building, the Labrador Heritage Museum (Portage Rd., 709/497-8858; June-Sept. daily 9am-5pm; $2 per person) provides an insight into Labrador's early years with photographs, manuscripts, books, artifacts, furs, native minerals, and other displays.

Accommodations

B&Bs offer the least-expensive lodgings. Davis' Bed and Breakfast (14 Cabot Cres., Happy Valley, 709/896-5077; $50-70 s, $70-90 d) has four guest rooms with private baths and wireless Internet. Rates include a continental breakfast (a full breakfast costs extra). Facilities include a dining room, laundry, and outside patio.

Happy Valley-Goose Bay has several motels catering mostly to business travelers. In general, rooms are of an acceptable standard and expensive, but not outrageously so. The Royal Inn and Suites (3 Royal Ave., Goose Bay, 709/896-2456 or 888/440-2456, www.royalinnandsuites.ca; $120-170 s, $130-180 d) is my pick of the bunch. It has 35 guest rooms, including a few with separate bedrooms, TV/DVD combos, and kitchens.

Rooms at the Labrador Inn (380 Hamilton River Rd., 709/896-3351 or 800/563-2763, www.labradorinn.nf.ca; $120-160) are of a similar standard. Facilities here include a restaurant, a lounge, and airport shuttles.

Food

Fast-food places line Hamilton River Road, including the ubiquitous and ever-popular Tim Hortons (220 Hamilton River Rd., 709/896-5666), a coffee-and-doughnut place.

The casual Jungle Jim's (Hotel North Two, 382 Hamilton River Rd., 709/896-3398; daily 11am-10pm; $13-27) features a menu of typical Canadian dishes. Next door in the Labrador Inn, Don Cherry's (380 Hamilton River Rd., 709/896-3351; daily 7am-2pm and 5pm-10pm; $14-26) is a modern sports bar with an extensive menu of standard pub fare at prices that are probably a bit higher than you want to pay.

Labrador Heritage Museum, North West River

The closest thing to a splurge in all of Labrador would be dinner at Bentley's (97 Hamilton River Rd., 709/896-3565; Mon.-Sat. 11am-9:30pm; $12-27), a semi-stylish, air-conditioned room overlooking the Churchill River. The food is fairly predictable, with the usual array of steak, chicken, pork, and sea-food dishes.

Information and Services

Destination Labrador (709/896-6507, www. destinationlabrador.com) operates a helpful information center along the main drag (365 Hamilton River Rd.; June-Sept. Mon.-Fri. 8am-8pm, Sat.-Sun. 8am-5pm).

Melville Hospital (also called Grenfell Hospital) is at Building 550, G Street (near 5th Avenue). For the RCMP (149 Hamilton River Rd.), call 709/896-3383. Post offices are located on Hamilton River Road and at the airport.

Getting There and Around

In 2010, the final link in the TransLabrador Highway was completed, and Goose Bay was linked to the rest of the province by road. The highway leading west to Churchill Falls (288 kilometers) was already in place, but the section leading south to the Labrador Straits was a much bigger undertaking for engineers (620 km to Blanc Sablon). To this day, much of the road is still unpaved and going can be ex-tremely slow, especially in spring before grad-ers have completed their work. But if you're up for an adventure, the journey along one of North America's newest and most remote highways is well worth considering.

Air Canada (888/247-2262) flies into Goose Bay Airport (YYR, www.goose-bayairport.com) from Halifax and Toronto. Air Labrador (709/758-0002 or 800/563-3042, www.airlabrador.com) flies be-tween Goose Bay and St. Anthony on Newfoundland's Northern Peninsula. Provincial Airlines (709/576-3943 or 800/563-2800, www.provincialairlines.ca) has flights to Goose Bay from as far away as Montreal and St. John's.

Budget (709/896-2973) and National (709/896-5575) have rental cars in town and out at the airport, but neither company allows its vehicles on the TransLabrador Highway. Deluxe Cabs (709/896-2424) charges around $8 per trip anywhere within Goose Bay, and $17 between the airport and Happy Valley.

CHURCHILL FALLS

Churchill Falls, 288 kilometers west of Goose Bay, is a relatively modern town constructed to serve the needs of workers at one of North America's largest hydroelectric schemes. The waters of the Churchill River drop more than 300 meters over a 32-kilometer section—ideal for generating hydroelectric power. In an incredible feat of engineering, the water is diverted underground to the massive gen-erators, which produce 5,220 megawatts of electricity.

The 21-room Midway Travel Inn (709/925-3211 or 800/229-3269, www.mid-waylabrador.ca; $154 s or d) is a modern lodg-ing attached to a restaurant (daily 7am-10pm) and the main town office complex. Rates in-clude use of an indoor pool, wireless Internet, and airport shuttles.

Getting There

To drive to Churchill Falls from Goose Bay, it's 290 kilometers (four hours) west via Route 500.

LABRADOR CITY AND WABUSH

Continuing west from Churchill Falls, the twin towns of Labrador City and Wabush, five kilometers apart, lie 530 kilometers from Goose Bay and just 23 kilometers from the Québec-Labrador border. Labradorians knew of the area's iron-ore potential by the late 1800s, and massive ore deposits were dis-covered in 1958. The Iron Ore Company of Canada and Wabush Mines, served by the two towns, together rank as the Canadian steel in-dustry's largest supplier. The two extract 20 million metric tons of iron ore a year.

Lodging in the two towns is limited to

Laying Claim to Labrador

For centuries the French Canadians have asserted, "Labrador is part of Québec." And the British and the Newfoundlanders have traditionally countered, "Never!"

Labrador is a choice piece of property, and Québec has been a longtime avid suitor of North America's northeastern edge. Québec's interest in Labrador dates to 1744, when the French cut a deal with the British: Québec got jurisdiction over Labrador, but the island of Newfoundland got fishing rights in Labrador's coastal waters. The Treaty of Paris of 1763 went one step further, however, and awarded all of Labrador (not defined by a precise border) to Newfoundland. Newfoundland's claim gained more substance in 1825, when the British North America Act set Labrador's southern border with Québec at the 52nd parallel.

In the 1860s, when the Dominion of Canada was formed, the dispute over Labrador, formerly between France and England, now involved the new Confederation of Canada. Québec never disputed England's sovereignty over Labrador, but instead continued to question the location of the border. In 1898 the Québec border was unofficially as far east as what is now the town of Happy Valley-Goose Bay.

FOR SALE: LABRADOR

Newfoundland put Labrador up for sale in 1909 for $9 million, but there were no takers. In the ensuing years, Labrador's precise border became a tedious issue for England, and so in 1927 a judicial committee in London set Labrador's border at the "height of the land," the watershed line separating the Atlantic Ocean from Ungava Bay, the current provincial border of today. In the decision, Labrador acquired the wedge-shaped "Labrador Trough," a delta area rich in iron ore deposits and rivers perfect for harnessing hydroelectric power.

QUÉBEC'S CLOUT EMERGES

The only road access to Labrador is through Québec, so it is no surprise that that province became a major player in Labrador's economy. Québec bought into Labrador's hydroelectric fortune in the early 1970s. Québec's provincial Hydro-Québec now earns $200 million annually from within Labrador, while Newfoundland, another company shareholder, earns $12 million. Ironically, Newfoundland and Labrador receive none of the energy.

To this day, the province's western border remains to be fully surveyed, and Québec does not consider the issue settled. A fragile status quo exists between the two provinces, but the renaming of Newfoundland to Newfoundland and Labrador in 2001 brought official recognition to Labrador as part of Newfoundland.

NUNATSIAVUT

In 2004, Labrador's Inuit people were successful in a land-claim process that took 30 years to come to fruition. Led by the Labrador Inuit Association (709/922-2942, www.nunatsiavut. com), the indigenous people now have special rights to 142,000 square kilometers of land that extend north from Lake Melville to Torngat Mountains National Park. The latter was established as part of the claim.

---

just over 100 rooms in three motels. The Wabush Hotel (9 Grenfell Dr., Wabush, 709/282-3221, www.wabushhotel.com; $115 s, $125 d) is an imposing property dating to the 1960s. The 68 rooms have been revamped a few times since, and services include a Chinese/Canadian buffet lunch and dinner in its restaurant and a convenience store.

Two Seasons Inn (96 Avalon Dr., Labrador City, 709/944-2661 or 800/670-7667, www. twoseasonsinn.ca; $130 s, $145 d) has the best 54 guest rooms in Labrador, airport shuttle service, a restaurant, and all the amenities of a big-city hotel.

At Duley Lake Family Park (10 km west of Labrador City, 709/282-3660; late

May-Sept.; $18), choose between campsites on either the lake or river. The campground has a sandy beach, boating, fishing, and picnicking. **Grande Hermine Park** (45 km east of Labrador City, 709/282-5369; June-Aug.; $18) offers 45 powered sites and 30 unserviced sites. Facilities include a boat launch, a convenience store, and pedal boat rentals.

Getting There

From Churchill Falls to Labrador City and Wabush, it's a 240-kilometer (3.5-hour) drive west on Route 500.

North Coast

Labrador's northern coast evokes images of another world. It's the Labrador you might imagine: raw and majestic, with the craggy mountain ranges of Torngat, Kaumajet, and Kiglapait rising to the north.

The 1763 Treaty of Paris ceded the Labrador coastline to Britain's Newfoundland colony, but the imprint of European architecture only reached the northern seacoast when the Moravians, an evangelical Protestant sect from Bohemia, established mission stations with prefabricated wooden buildings in the early 19th century. It is in these remote north coast villages—Rigolet, Postville, Makkovik, and Nain—that the original inhabitants, the Inuit, have settled. Few aspects of these towns have changed over the last century, and the lifestyle of northern peoples here remains traditional.

Getting There

Access to Labrador's north coast is by air or sea. The communities are linked to the outside world by **Air Labrador** (709/753-5593 or 800/563-3042, www.airlabrador.com) from Goose Bay, or by a cargo and passenger ferry that takes two days to reach its northern turnaround point, Nain. Riding the ferry, the **MV *Northern Ranger,*** is a real adventure. The one-way fare for an adult between Goose Bay and Nain is $160. A single berth in a shared cabin costs $80, while a private cabin costs from $300 to $630 s or d. For more

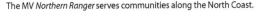
The MV *Northern Ranger* serves communities along the North Coast.

information, call 800/563-6353. The website www.labradorferry.ca lists a schedule and prices.

MAKKOVIK

After stopping at Rigolet, the MV *Northern Ranger* starts its long haul through open ocean, reaching Makkovik (pop. 400) 18 hours after leaving Goose Bay. The ferry makes a 90-minute stop on the way north and a three-hour stop on the return journey. Makkovik was first settled in the early 1800s by a Norwegian fur trader; the Moravians constructed a mission here in 1896. Today this two-story building holds the White Elephant Museum (709/923-2425, July-Aug. daily 1pm-5pm, or by appointment). Local shops such as the Makkovik Craft Centre (709/923-2221, call for hours) sell Inuit crafts, including fur caps, boots and mittens, parkas, moose-hide moccasins, and bone and antler jewelry.

Right on the water, the Adlavik Inn (7 Willow Creek Ln., 709/923-2389, www.labradorabletours.com; $120 s, $150 d) has the only five guest rooms in town, so call ahead if your itinerary includes an overnight stay in Makkovik. Rooms have TVs and phones, and meals are served in an adjacent dining room.

HOPEDALE

About 110 nautical miles north of Makkovik and 122 miles short of Nain, the MV *Northern Ranger* makes a two-hour stop at Hopedale, just enough time to go ashore and visit the 1782 Hopedale Mission National Historic Site (709/933-3864; adult $5), containing the oldest wooden frame building east of Québec. Here, a restored Hudson's Bay Company storeroom has been converted into a museum; other site highlights include huts, a residence, and a graveyard. It generally opens whenever the ferry is in town.

Accommodations are provided at Amaguk Inn (709/933-3750, www.labradoradventures. com), which charges $130 s, $155 d for its 18 rooms. Meals are available at the inn for both guests and nonguests.

NAIN AND THE FAR NORTH

With stunning coastal scenery, stops at remote villages, and the chance to see whales and icebergs, the long trip north aboard the MV *Northern Ranger* ferry is a real adventure, but after two days on board, the captain's announcement of imminent arrival in Nain, administrative capital of Nunatsiavut, is welcome. In the early 1900s, an epidemic of Spanish flu—introduced from a supply ship—destroyed a third of the indigenous population on the northern coast. The Inuit who survived resettled at Nain, which now has a population of just over 1,000 and is the northernmost municipality on the Labrador coast. Life is rugged this far north—electricity is provided by diesel generator; fuel and wood are used for domestic heat; local transportation is by boat in the summer and snowmobile in the winter. The only roads are within the town itself.

Accommodations and Food

For an overnight stay, there's just one option, the Atsanik Lodge (Sand Banks Rd., 709/922-2910; $145 s, $155 d). Each of the 25 rooms has cable TV, a phone, and a private bathroom. The lodge also has a lounge, restaurant, and laundry. Other town services include a couple of grocery stores, a post office, and a takeout food joint.

Getting There

If you've arrived on the ferry, you'll have just three hours ashore to explore the town before the return journey. The alternative is to take the ferry one way and an Air Labrador (709/753-5593 or 800/563-3042) flight the other. The one-way fare to Goose Bay is around $480.

Voisey's Bay

Prior to the cod-fishing moratorium, the fishing industry dominated Labrador's Far North Coast, but now mining at Voisey Bay, 35 kilometers south, appears to be the economic engine of the future. It is home to world's largest known deposit of nickel and copper. The main processing facility was completed in early 2006, and now around 6,000 tons of nickel and copper concentrate are mined daily by over 400 workers.

Hebron Mission National Historic Site

Labrador's northernmost remaining Moravian mission is protected at Hebron Mission National Historic Site, on the shores of remote Kangershutsoak Bay, 140 nautical miles north of Nain. Building began on the mission complex, including a church, residence, and store, in 1829. The mission remained in operation until 1959. Nature Trek Canada (250/653-4265, www.naturetrek.ca) can make a stop here on its custom guided tours along the northern Labrador coastline.

★ Torngat Mountains National Park

Established in 2006 as part of the Nunatsiavut land claim, the remote wilderness of Torngat Mountains National Park protects 9,700 square kilometers of the remote coastline and rugged Torngat Mountains at the northern tip of Labrador. Glaciation dominates the park's geology; its mountains are separated by deep fiords and lakes that have been carved by retreating glaciers, many of which are still present in pockets scattered through the park. The entire park is above the treeline, so instead of trees, its valleys are carpeted in a variety of tundra vegetation, including wildflowers, which carpet large expanses during the very short summer season. Huge herds of caribou migrate across the park's interior, while polar bears are common along the coast.

Unless you are a long-distance kayaker, the only way to reach the park is by charter flight from Goose Bay to Saglek and then a boat transfer into the park. Flights and all ground services are arranged by Torngat Mountains Base Camp (855/867-6428, www.torngatbasecamp.com). Owned by the Labrador Inuit Development Corporation and with a season extending from mid-July to early September, this company's on-site camp is at the south end of the park. Although used mostly by park staff and researchers, the facility also offers a variety of services for park visitors. Expect to pay around $4,000 for flights from Happy Valley-Goose Bay, the boat transfer, tent accommodation for four nights, meals, and limited guiding.

The main park office (709/922-1290; Mon.-Fri. 9am-4:30pm) is in Nain, although the best source of information for planning your trip is www.pc.gc.ca/torngat, where you can download a visitors' guide and hiking maps.

Torngat Mountains Base Camp

Photo Credits

MAP SYMBOLS

≡≡≡	Expressway	○	City/Town	✈	Airport	⚓	Golf Course
—	Primary Road	◉	State Capital	✈	Airfield	🅿	Parking Area
—	Secondary Road	⊛	National Capital	▲	Mountain	⬭	Archaeological Site
- - -	Unpaved Road	★	Point of Interest	✚	Unique Natural Feature	⬛	Church
—	Feature Trail	•	Accommodation		Waterfall	🛢	Gas Station
- - - - -	Other Trail	▼	Restaurant/Bar	♠	Park		Glacier
··········	Ferry	■	Other Location	⬛	Trailhead		Mangrove
	Pedestrian Walkway	Λ	Campground	⛷	Skiing Area		Reef
⊐⊐⊐⊐⊐	Stairs						Swamp

CONVERSION TABLES

°C = (°F − 32) / 1.8
°F = (°C x 1.8) + 32
1 inch = 2.54 centimeters (cm)
1 foot = 0.304 meters (m)
1 yard = 0.914 meters
1 mile = 1.6093 kilometers (km)
1 km = 0.6214 miles
1 fathom = 1.8288 m
1 chain = 20.1168 m
1 furlong = 201.168 m
1 acre = 0.4047 hectares
1 sq km = 100 hectares
1 sq mile = 2.59 square km
1 ounce = 28.35 grams
1 pound = 0.4536 kilograms
1 short ton = 0.90718 metric ton
1 short ton = 2,000 pounds
1 long ton = 1.016 metric tons
1 long ton = 2,240 pounds
1 metric ton = 1,000 kilograms
1 quart = 0.94635 liters
1 US gallon = 3.7854 liters
1 Imperial gallon = 4.5459 liters
1 nautical mile = 1.852 km

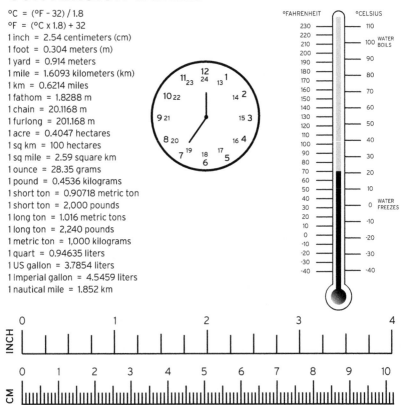

MOON SPOTLIGHT
NEWFOUNDLAND & LABRADOR

Avalon Travel
a member of the Perseus Books Group
1700 Fourth Street
Berkeley, CA 94710, USA
www.moon.com

Editor: Leah Gordon
Series Manager: Kathryn Ettinger
Copy Editor: Kristie Reilly
Graphics Coordinators: Kathryn Osgood,
 Elizabeth Jang
Production Coordinator: Elizabeth Jang
Cover Design: Faceout Studios, Charles Brock
Moon Logo: Tim McGrath
Map Editor: Kat Bennett
Cartographers: Brian Shotwell, Stephanie Poulain

ISBN-13: 978-1-63121-128-7

Front cover photo: fishing village in Newfoundland
© Chiyacat/istockphoto.com

Printed in the United States

All recommendations, including those for sights,
activities, hotels, restaurants, and shops, are based
on each author's individual judgment. We do not
accept payment for inclusion in our travel guides,
and our authors don't accept free goods or services
in exchange for positive coverage.

Although every effort was made to ensure that
the information was correct at the time of going
to press, the author and publisher do not assume
and hereby disclaim any liability to any party for any
loss or damage caused by errors, omissions, or any
potential travel disruption due to labor or financial
difficulty, whether such errors or omissions result
from negligence, accident, or any other cause.

About the Author

Andrew Hempstead

© DIANNE MELTON

As a professional travel writer, Andrew spends as much time as possible out on the road. During his travels, he experiences the many and varied delights of Newfoundland and Labrador the same way his readers do.

Since the early 1990s, Andrew has authored and updated more than 60 guidebooks, and supplied content for regional and national clients like Expedia and KLM. His photography has appeared in a wide variety of media, ranging from international golf magazines to a Ripley's Believe it or Not! Museum.

Andrew and his wife Dianne own Summerthought Publishing, a Canadian regional publisher of nonfiction books. He is a member of The Diners Club® World's 50 Best Restaurants Academy. Andrew has also spoken on travel writing to a national audience and has contributed to a university-level travel writing textbook.

CPSIA information can be obtained
at www.ICGtesting.com
Printed in the USA
LVOW02s2136090616
491555LV00026B/37/P